Small Batch Baking Cookbook

Cakes, Cookies, Muffins, and More Made for Smaller Households

Antonio Bruns

Table of Content

Introduction 4
(Breads And Biscuits Recipes) 6
1. Small Batch Homemade Biscuits 6
2. Buttermilk Biscuits 7
3. Small Batch Drop Biscuits 8
4. Cream Cheese Sugar Cookies 9
5. Salted Butter Chocolate Chunk Shortbread Cookies 10
6. Quick Yeast Bread 11
7. Low Carb Bread (Almond Flour Bread) 12
8. Chocolate Chip Cookies 13
9. Basic Biscuits Recipes 14
10. Pumpkin Muffins With Crumb Topping 15
11. Best Half-batch Chocolate Chip Cookies 16
12. Ketogenic Biscuits 17
13. Zero Carb Bread - Egg White Protein Bread 18
14. Small Batch Monkey Bread 19
15. Small Batch Crusty Bread 20
16. Small Batch Buttermilk Biscuits 21
17. Garlic Parmesan Pull-Apart Bread (small batch) 23
18. Easy Drop Biscuits 24
19. Simple & Classic Shortbread 25
20. Granny's Monkey Bread Recipe 26
(Muffins And Cupcakes Recipes) 27
21. Chocolate Chip Muffins 27
22. Small Batch Blueberry Muffin Recipe 28
23. Chocolate Cream Cheese Muffins 30
24. Small Batch Vanilla Cupcakes 31
25. Small-Batch Chocolate Chip Muffins 32
26. Small Batch One Banana Muffins 33
27. Moist Small Batch Lemon Blueberry Muffins 35
28. Plain Muffin Recipe 36
29. Small Batch Carrot Cake 37
30. Mini Pound Cake 38
31. Banana Chocolate Chip Muffins with Streusel 39
32. Small Batch Banana Muffins 41
33. Homemade Blueberry Muffin Recipe 42
34. Basic muffin recipe 43
35. Coffee Cake Muffins 44
36. Healthier Chocolate Chip Muffin 45
37. Best Ever Muffins 46
38. Ultimate Muffins Recipe 47
39. Pumpkin Gingerbread Muffins 48
40. Cinnamon Muffins 49
(Cookies, Browinies And Bars Recipes) 51
41. Small-batch Sugar Cookies 51
42. PB&J Thumbprint Cookies 52
43. Small-Batch Snickerdoodles (Thick and Soft) 53
44. Double Chocolate Cookies 55
45. Peanut Butter Cookies Recipe 56

46. Small Batch Almond Joy Cookies	57
47. Small Batch Butter Cookies	58
48. Small Batch Triple Chocolate Cookies	59
49. vegan chocolate chip cookies	60
50. Oatmeal Cookies with Icing	61
51. Easiest Small Batch Chocolate Chip Cookies With Brown Butter And Sea Salt	62
52. Small Batch No Bake Cookies	64
53. Best Oatmeal Chocolate Chip Cookies	65
54. Chocolate Chip Walnut Cookies	66
55. Peppermint Bark Cookies	67
56. Caramel Pecan Thumbprint Cookies	68
57. Chocolate Crinkle Cookies	70
58. Small Batch Ricotta Cookies	71
59. Small Batch of Sugar Cookies	72
60. Small-batch Peanut Butter Cookies	73
(Bars Recipes)	75
61. Small Batch Brookie Bars Recipe	75
62. Homemade Lemon Bars (Easy Lemon Bar Recipe)	77
63. Small Batch Magic Cookie Bars Recipe	78
64. Small Batch Peanut Butter Bars	80
65. Mini-batch Twix Bars	81
66. Chocolate Chunk Cookie Bars	82
67. Peanut Butter Bars Recipe	83
68. Chocolate Chip Cookie Bars	84
69. Small Batch Lemon Bars	85
70. Magic Cookie Bars, Small Batch	86
71. Sugar Cookie Bars with Cream Cheese	87
72. Small Batch Blondies	88
73. Seriously Fudgy Small Batch Brownies	89
74. Small-batch Monster Cookie Bars	91
75. Small Batch Jam Crumble Bars	92
76. Mini-batch Snickers Bars	93
77. Monster Cookie Bars	94
78. Grain-Free and Sugar-Free Magic Cookie Bars	95
79. Healthy Pumpkin Chocolate Chip Oat Bars (vegan and gluten free)	96
(Pies, Tarts, And Quiche Recipes)	98
80. Small Batch Pumpkin Pie	98
81. Small Pie Crust (6 Inch Pie Pan)	100
82. Small-batch Whoopie Pies	101
83. Mini Pecan Pies (Mini Muffin Pan)	103
84. Mini Pie Crust	104
85. Mini Pumpkin Pies	105
86. Apple Pie From Scratch	106
87. Easy Mini Apple Pies	108
88. Apple Hand Pies	109
89. Pecan Butter Tarts	110
90. Mini Fruit Tarts with Vanilla Pastry Cream	111
91. Tiny Pecan Tarts	113
92. Miniature Bakewell Tarts	114
93. Mini Tart Shells Recipe	116

94. Mini Quiche Recipe	117
95. Crustless Quiche	118
96. Chocolate Chip Cookie Recipe	119
97. Spaghetti Pie	120
98. Mini Dutch Apple Pies	122
99. Pineapple Tarts Recipe	123
(Puddings Recipes)	124
100. Easy Chocolate Pudding	124
101. Yorkshire puddings recipes	125
102. Bread Pudding	126
103. Easy Rice Pudding	127
104. Banana Pudding (From Scratch)	128
105. Vanilla Pudding recipes	129
106. Small Batch Cheesecake	130
107. Apple Turnovers	131
108. Small Batch Brown Butter Chocolate Chip Cookies	132
109. Small Batch Muddy Buddies Recipe	133
110. Easy Small Batch Focaccia	134
111. Small Batch Brownies Recipe	135
112. Easy small batch brownies recipe	136
113. Small Batch Chex Mix	137
114. Peanut Butter Energy Balls (aka Quick and Healthy Snack Bites)	138
115. Small-batch Vanilla Cupcakes	139
116. Small-batch Vanilla Cake	140
117. Hot Milk Sponge Cake	141
118. Small Chocolate Cake	142
119. Coconut Cookie Bars	144

INTRODUCTION

For anyone who loves baking but finds themselves needing just a small taste rather than an entire tray or a towering cake, Small Batch Baking Cookbook is here to bring the joy of homemade treats to smaller households. With recipes specifically designed for one to four servings, this cookbook delivers the satisfaction of fresh-baked goodness without the excess. Whether you're cooking for two, embracing single-serve indulgence, or simply wanting less cleanup, this book offers the ideal balance between quality and portion control.

Why Small Batch Baking?

Baking in smaller quantities is about more than portion size; it's about capturing that "fresh out of the oven" magic each time you bake. Unlike traditional recipes that yield large quantities, these small-batch creations allow you to bake a treat when the craving strikes—without leftover temptation. Imagine a single, perfectly baked mini pie or a few warm cookies to savor without guilt. With small-batch baking, you're free to experiment with new flavors and recipes every week without worrying about food waste or overflowing dessert trays.

Perfect for Every Skill Level

Whether you're a seasoned baker or just starting out, the Small Batch Baking Cookbook simplifies the process with easy-to-follow recipes that scale down effortlessly. These recipes don't just cut ingredients in half—they're crafted to ensure that flavor, texture, and presentation are just as delightful as any full-sized bake. Beginners will appreciate the simplicity, while experienced bakers will enjoy the challenge of creating beautifully small treats that pack big flavor.

A Versatile Collection of Recipes

Inside this book, you'll find a range of delightful recipes from every baking category.

- **Breads and Biscuits:** Start your day with homemade small-batch biscuits or a mini loaf of fresh bread. Perfect for cozy breakfasts or a savory snack, these recipes include everything from crusty bread to garlic pull-apart rolls.
- **Muffins and Cupcakes:** Brighten up your mornings or snack times with freshly baked muffins in flavors like blueberry, chocolate chip, and pumpkin spice. Small-batch cupcakes add a touch of celebration to any day with minimal effort.
- **Cookies, Brownies, and Bars:** Craving a cookie? Choose from classic chocolate chip, snickerdoodles, and even caramel thumbprint cookies, all scaled down to small, satisfying portions. For brownie and bar lovers, indulge in chewy, fudgy small-batch brownies and easy, no-bake bars.
- **Pies, Tarts, and Quiches:** From mini apple pies to single-serve quiches, these recipes are a treat for any time of day. Enjoy a comforting dessert or a savory quiche for brunch, all tailored to satisfy without the need for sharing (unless you want to!).
- **Puddings and Custards:** Finish off your meal with a creamy, comforting pudding or custard recipe. From rich chocolate pudding to vanilla-infused custards, each recipe is made with just enough to enjoy in the moment.

Baking Tips and Tricks for Small Batches

In addition to recipes, this cookbook provides a wealth of tips for small-batch success. Learn how to adapt baking times and temperatures, measure ingredients with precision, and get creative with substitutions. You'll also find advice on selecting the best tools and bakeware for small-batch baking, so you can achieve the best results with minimal fuss.

A Fresh Approach to Satisfy Any Craving

Small Batch Baking Cookbook: Cakes, Cookies, Muffins, and More Made for Smaller Households brings you the joy of baking on your terms. Every recipe is designed to yield just enough for a treat, leaving you free to explore flavors and try new things. It's the perfect solution for anyone looking to enjoy the pleasures of homemade baked goods without the hassle of leftovers. Discover the joy of baking just for you (or a lucky someone) with recipes that are as fun to make as they are delicious to eat.

(BREADS AND BISCUITS RECIPES)

1. SMALL BATCH HOMEMADE BISCUITS

Prep Time: 10 Mins

Cook Time: 12 Mins

Total Time: 22 Mins

Serving: 5

Ingredients

- 1 cup of all-purpose flour + extra for dusting and cutting
- 1 tsp baking powder
- ¾ tsp kosher salt
- 1 ½ tsp granulated sugar
- 3 tbsp cold, unsalted butter
- ½ cup of cold, whole milk

Instructions

1. Warm the oven to 425 °F. Use parchment paper to line a small baking sheet.
2. In a big bowl, whisk together the dried ingredients.
3. Cut the cold butter into ½" cubes and add them directly to the dry ingredients. Crumble the cool butter into the dry ingredients with your hands until it forms a coarse crumb.
4. Using a fork, gently whisk in the whole milk until the dough forms a rough ball. (Add another tbsp flour if the dough appears too moist).
5. Turn the rough dough out onto a thoroughly floured surface. Stretch it out slowly into a rectangle that is about an inch thick.
6. Fold the front half of the rectangle over the bottom half, then gently pat down again. Fold the dough again in half, but this time, fold the right side over the left.
7. Repeat the folds from the previous step gently. (Fold in half front to back, pat down lightly, and then fold in half side to side.) Form it gently into a rectangle about one inch thick.
8. In the additional flour, dip a 2-inch biscuit cutter. Press down hard on the dough as you cut it into two biscuits. To release the biscuits from the dough, softly wiggle the cutter back and forth, but do not twist it.
9. Form the remaining dough into a one-inch-thick rectangle, then cut out the third and fourth biscuits. Put the biscuits about ½" apart on the prepared baking sheet.

10. Bake the biscuits at 425 °F for twelve to fourteen minutes or until the tops are golden brown.
11. Take from the oven, and let the biscuits rest until they are cool enough to handle. Enjoy!

2. BUTTERMILK BISCUITS

Prep Time: 25 Mins

Cook Time: 10 Mins

Total Time: 35 Mins

Serving: 8

Ingredients

- 1⅓ cups of flour
- ½ tsp salt
- 1½ tsp baking powder
- ⅛ tsp baking soda
- 4 tbsp chilled unsalted butter
- ½ cup of buttermilk plus extra if needed

Instructions

1. Warm the oven to 450 degrees and line a quarter-sheet baking pan with parchment paper.
2. In a small bowl, stir together the baking soda, flour, salt, and baking powder.
3. Sliced the butter into small pieces and add it to the flour combination, slicing it in with a pastry cutter or two knives.
4. Once all the fat pieces are about the size of rice and covered in flour, add the buttermilk. Knead it lightly, then add one tsp buttermilk at a time if the biscuit dough appears dry or crumbly. However, avoid adding more buttermilk because the wetter the dough, the less the biscuits will rise in the oven.
5. Turn the dough out onto a floured surface and knead it three or four times to bring it together.
6. Pat it out to 1" thickness. Cut out four biscuits with your 3" biscuit or cookie cutter after dipping it in flour. To cut out two more biscuits, gather the scraps and gently pat them out.

7. Put the biscuits on the pan so that they are evenly spaced. Lightly golden on top, bake for nine to ten minutes. If you choose, brush them with more melted butter as they come out of the oven.

3. SMALL BATCH DROP BISCUITS

Prep Time: 5 Mins

Cook Time: 12 Mins

Total Time: 17 Mins

Serving: 4

Ingredients

- 1 cup of all-purpose flour
- 1 tsp baking powder
- 1 tsp sugar
- ½ tsp salt
- 3 tbsp cold salted butter (cut into ¼-inch pieces)
- ½ cup of milk

Instructions

1. Warm the oven to 400 degrees Fahrenheit, and line a baking sheet with parchment paper.
2. In a big bowl, stir together sugar, flour, baking powder, and salt.
3. Combine the butter with the dry ingredients. Rub or chop the butter into the flour with a pastry blender or your fingertips until the mixture resembles gritty sand.
4. Pour in the milk and whisk just until the dough comes together.
5. Drop spoonsful of batter onto a cooking sheet and bake until golden brown, about ten to twelve minutes.

4. CREAM CHEESE SUGAR COOKIES

Prep Time: 25 Mins

Cook Time: 10 Mins

Total Time: 25 Mins

Serving: 24

Ingredients

- 6 cups + 4 tbsp all-purpose flour
- 1 tbsp baking powder
- 1 tsp salt
- 2 cups of unsalted cubed, soften butter
- 8 Ounces soften cream cheese
- 2 cups of white sugar
- 2 eggs
- 1 tbsp vanilla extract

Directions

1. Sift dry ingredients in a medium bowl: six cups of plus four tbsp of all-purpose flour, one tbsp of baking powder, and one tsp of salt. Set aside
2. In a standing kitchen blender with the paddle attachment, cream eight ounces of softened cream cheese, two cups of soften cubed unsalted butter, and two cups of white sugar until super light and creamy. Approximately ten to twelve minutes.
3. Stop blender and scrape those sides 3x once mixing. This aids in the combination of sugar and fat.
4. In a small bowl, stir two eggs and one tbsp of vanilla. Gently add it while the mixer is on low speed.
5. Stop and scrape the sides.
6. Mix in the dry ingredients for thirty to forty-five seconds or until just combined.
7. If preparing a drop cookie, scoop the dough and roll it in demerara sugar or sprinkles. Bake at 350° for ten to twelve minutes.
8. If making cutouts, cover the dough in plastic wrap and refrigerate for about two hours or overnight.
9. Roll the flour to ¼ inch thickness on a rolling mat. Cut with your preferred cookie cutters. Bake at 350° for eight to twelve minutes, depending on shape.
10. Cool completely prior to frosting.

5. SALTED BUTTER CHOCOLATE CHUNK SHORTBREAD COOKIES

Prep Time: 2 Hrs 15 Mins

Cook Time: 15 Mins

Total Time: 2 Hrs 30 Mins

Serving: 40

Ingredients

- 1 cup plus two tbsp cold salted butter (cut into ½" pieces)
- ½ cup of sugar
- ¼ cup of packed light brown sugar
- 1 tsp vanilla
- 2¼ cups of all-purpose flour
- 6 ounces bittersweet or semisweet dark chocolate (chopped into chunks)
- flaky sea salt

Instructions

1. Use an electric stand blender with the paddle attachment or a hand blender to mix the cold butter, sugars, and vanilla for about three to five minutes or until the mixture is light and fluffy.
2. Scrape down the edges, then gradually add the flour. Combine just until mixed, then add the chocolate and mix just until combined.
3. Split the dough in half, then set each half on a wide piece of plastic wrap. Roll into a log. Allow to chill for two hours.
4. At this point, cookies can be wrapped and refrigerated for up to a week or frozen for up to a month. Slice ½ inch thick and bake.
5. Warm oven to 350° and bake on cookie sheets coated with parchment paper for twelve to fifteen minutes.

6. QUICK YEAST BREAD

Total Time: 1 Hr 20 Mins

Serving: 2

Ingredients

- 5 cups of all-purpose white flour
- 2 tbsp yeast
- 2 tsp sugar
- 1 tsp salt
- 2 cups of warm-hot water
- ¼ cup of cooking oil

Directions

1. In a large bowl, put four cups of flour, yeast, sugar, and salt.
2. Put in boiling water and oil and mix until mixed- it will be sticky.
3. Put the remaining flour slowly until the dough is no longer sticky.
4. Knead the dough for about five minutes until it is elastic and smooth.
5. Return the dough to the bowl, cover it with a wet tea towel, and let it to rise for approximately half an hour or until it doubles in size.
6. Punch it down and split the dough into two pieces.
7. Roll out sections long enough to fill two well-oiled loaf pans and let rise until the dough reaches the rim of the pan.
8. Bake at 400°F for forty minutes.
9. Rub heated bread with water and wrap it in a tea towel to 'sweat' to soften the crust.

7. LOW CARB BREAD (ALMOND FLOUR BREAD)

Prep Time: 10 Mins

Cook Time: 1 Hr

Total Time: 1 Hr 10 Mins

Serving: 18

Ingredients

- 2 cups of wholesome yum blanched almond flour
- ¼ cup of psyllium husk powder
- 1 tbsp baking powder
- ½ tsp sea salt
- 4 big eggs at room temperature
- ¼ cup of coconut oil (measured solid, then melted)
- ½ cup of warm water

Instructions

1. Set the oven's temperature to 350° Fahrenheit (177°C). Line the bottom of an 8-by-4-inch loaf pans with parchment paper.
2. Use a hand blender on high speed to beat the eggs in a big bowl until they double in size.
3. Put the psyllium husk powder, baking powder, and sea salt in a second big bowl and mix them together.
4. Combine the dry ingredients with the eggs.
5. Add the warm water and then beat in the melted coconut oil.
6. In a lined baking pan, move the dough. Smooth/press the top evenly with your hands or a spatula to form a rounded shape.
7. Bake for 55-70 minutes, or until the tip of a toothpick inserted into the very middle comes out clean and the top is extremely firm, like a bread crust. (Important: it will pass the toothpick test before it's totally done, so make sure the top is also crusty.) Let it cool fully prior to removing it from the pan.

8. CHOCOLATE CHIP COOKIES

Prep Time: 15 Mins

Cook Time: 12 Mins

Chilling Time: 10 Mins

Total Time: 37 Mins

Servings: 10

Ingredients

- ¼ cup of unsalted softened butter
- ¼ cup of packed light brown sugar
- 2 tbsp granulated sugar
- 1 big egg yolk at room temperature
- ½ tsp pure vanilla extract
- ½ cup plus 1 tbsp all-purpose flour (spooned & leveled)
- ¼ tsp baking soda
- ½ cup of semi-sweet chocolate chips
- ¼ tsp salt

Instructions

1. Set the oven temp to 350 degrees F, or 177°C. Put parchment paper or a silicone cooking mat on a big baking sheet and put it aside.
2. In a mixing bowl of medium size, using an electric blender, beat the brown sugar, butter, and granulated sugar together for one to two minutes or until well mixed.
3. As necessary, scrape the bowl's sides down as you stir in the egg yolk and vanilla extract until thoroughly combined.
4. Combine with the salt, baking soda, and flour until it's just mixed. Then, add the semisweet chocolate chips and mix on low speed until they are fully mixed into the dough.
5. Cover tightly and move to the freezer to chill for ten minutes.
6. Using a 1.5 tbsp cookie scoop, transfer the cookie dough to the prepared baking sheet, leaving a little space between each.
7. Bake for ten to twelve minutes or until the edges of the cookies are softly golden brown and the tops have set.
8. Take the cookies out of the oven and let them cool for about five to ten minutes on the baking sheet. Then, move them to a wire rack to cool all the way through.

9. BASIC BISCUITS RECIPES

Prep Time: 15 Mins

Cook Time: 10 Mins

Total Time: 25 Mins

Servings: 10

Ingredients

- 2 cups of all-purpose flour
- 1 tbsp baking powder
- ½ cup of shortening
- ½ tsp salt
- ¾ cup of cold milk

Directions

1. Gather all of the ingredients and warm the oven to 450 degrees F (230°C).
2. In a big bowl, sift the baking powder, flour, and salt. Slice in the shortening with a fork or pastry blender until the combination resembles coarse crumbs.
3. Put the milk into the flour combination, stirring with a fork. Combine in the milk until the dough is soft and wet and pulls away from the sides of the bowl.
4. Move the flour to a lightly floured surface and knead briefly five to seven times.
5. Roll out the flour to ½ inch thickness and use a floured cookie cutter to cut out the biscuits. Press together any extra dough, and then roll and cut it again.
6. Bake the biscuits on ungreased baking sheets for about ten minutes or until they are golden brown.
7. Enjoy!

10. PUMPKIN MUFFINS WITH CRUMB TOPPING

Prep Time: 20 Mins

Cook Time: 25 Mins

Total Time: 45 Mins

Servings: 6

Ingredients

For the Muffins

- 1 cup of all-purpose flour
- ½ tsp baking soda
- ½ tsp cinnamon
- pinch of cloves
- dash of salt
- ½ cup of unflavored melted coconut oil
- ¼ cup of sugar
- ¼ cup of brown sugar
- ¾ cup of canned pumpkin puree
- 1 egg
- ¼ cup of sour cream

For the Crumb Topping

- ½ cup of all-purpose flour
- 3 tbsp sugar
- 3 tbsp brown sugar
- ⅛ tsp cinnamon
- 3 tbsp unsalted melted butter

For the Glaze

- ¾ cup of confectioners' sugar
- 2 tbsp milk

Directions

1. Warm the oven to 350 degrees Fahrenheit. Line a muffin pan with six muffin liners and lightly oil. Set aside.
2. **For the Muffins:** Mix together the flour, baking soda, cloves, cinnamon, and salt in a big bowl, then set it aside.
3. In a medium bowl, mix egg, pumpkin puree, coconut oil, brown sugar, and sour cream, stirring until well blended. Next, add the pumpkin combination to the flour combination and gently fold with a big rubber tip spatula until combined. Put the batter into the muffin tin that has been prepared. To flatten, gently tap the pan on the counter. Set aside.
4. **For the Crumb Topping:** Mix together the brown sugar, flour, sugar, and cinnamon in a small bowl until well combined. Put the melted butter and mix it in slowly with a fork until crumbs form. Be careful not to overmix. Split the crumb topping among the muffins and gently press it into the batter.
5. Put the muffins in the oven for about 21-25 minutes, or until a toothpick inserted into the middle comes out clean. Let the muffins to cool completely prior to glazing.
6. **For the Glaze:** Combine the milk and confectioners' sugar in a small bowl and stir until smooth. Sprinkle over the muffins and serve.

11. BEST HALF-BATCH CHOCOLATE CHIP COOKIES

Total Time: 15 Mins

Servings: 10-12

Ingredients

- 1 cup of flour, plus
- 2 tbsp flour
- ½ cup of butter
- 1 large egg
- ½ tsp salt
- 6 tbsp firmly packed brown sugar
- ½ tsp baking powder
- 6 tbsp granulated sugar
- ½ tsp vanilla extract
- ¾ cup of white chocolate chips
- ¾ cup of milk chocolate chips
- 2-3 tbsp cocoa powder (optional)

Directions

1. Use a medium speed to mix the butter and sugar.
2. While mixing, add the vanilla.
3. While mixing, add one egg.
4. Turn the blender off and add the flour.
5. Next, add salt.
6. Next, add baking powder.
7. Beat on low to medium speed until the flour is well integrated into the butter and sugar combination.
8. Carefully whisk in chocolate chips.
9. If you prefer chocolate or chocolate chip cookies, you may add cocoa powder to make them even better!
10. Shape into balls with two spoons and place on a baking stone or cookie sheet.
11. Bake at 375° for approximately seven minutes.
12. Take from the oven when the edges are just brown for a tender, moist cookie.
13. Let to set for a few minutes, if you can wait, or your cookie will fall apart.

12. KETOGENIC BISCUITS

Prep Time: 10 Mins

Cook Time: 15 Mins

Total Time: 25 Mins

Servings: 12

Ingredients

- 2 cups of wholesome yum blanched almond flour
- 2 tsp baking powder
- ½ tsp sea salt
- 2 large whisked eggs
- ⅓ cup of unsalted butter (measured solid, then melted)
- ¼ cup of sour cream (optional)

Instructions

1. Set the oven's temperature to 350° Fahrenheit (177 degrees Celsius). Use parchment paper to line a cooking sheet.

2. In a big bowl, mix dry almond flour, baking powder, and sea salt. Whisk in the whisked egg, melted butter, and optional sour cream.
3. The fastest way to do this is to use a cookie scoop to put tbspfuls of dough on the baking sheet that has been lined. Form into spherical biscuits (slightly flatten with your fingertips).
4. Bake for about fifteen minutes or until golden and firm. Cool on the baking sheet.

13. ZERO CARB BREAD - EGG WHITE PROTEIN BREAD

Prep Time: 10 Mins

Cook Time: 33 Mins

Total Time: 43 Mins

Servings: 16

Ingredients

- 12 fresh egg whites separated from yolks
- ¾ tsp sea salt
- 5 tbsp powdered monk fruit sweetener
- ½ tsp cream of tartar (optional)
- 1 cup of egg white protein

Instructions

1. Warm the oven to 325º F. Use parchment paper to line a 9×5 loaf pan. I first spray it with oil, then apply the parchment to help it cling to the pan, and then press the paper firmly against the sides. Set aside the prepared pan.
2. In a standing blender with a whisk attachment, combine fresh egg whites, cream of tartar, monk fruit sweetener, and salt. Stir on medium speed until the egg whites' foam, then increase to high speed until the egg whites form extremely firm peaks. Once the bowl is turned upside down, the egg whites should stay in place!
3. Put the egg white protein powder and mix well on low.
4. Add the egg white combination to the lined loaf pan. Use a spatula to mold the egg whites into a bread loaf.
5. Bake the bread for thirty-three minutes or until the top is a deep golden brown.
6. Let the bread cool thoroughly prior to slicing it.

14. SMALL BATCH MONKEY BREAD

Prep Time: 10 Mins

Cook Time: 40 Mins

Total Time: 50 Mins

Servings: 4

Ingredients

- ½ cup of granulated sugar
- 1 ½ tsp ground cinnamon
- 1 can store-bought biscuit dough
- 1 stick melted butter

Instructions

1. Warm the oven to 350 degrees Fahrenheit.
2. Combine the white sugar and cinnamon in a medium bowl and set aside.
3. Open your biscuit can or cans and cut them into four pieces each. After that, roll each piece into a ball, leaving you with biscuit pieces.
4. Toss the dough balls with the cinnamon sugar.
5. Warm the butter in a small bowl (I do this in the microwave at 30-second intervals).
6. In your 8 by 5-inch loaf pan, begin to layer the melted butter, dough balls, and remaining sugar combination.
7. Do this over and over until you've used up all the butter, dough balls, and cinnamon sugar.
8. Bake for forty minutes. Let to cool for twenty minutes prior to releasing by turning the pan upside down and digging in!

15. SMALL BATCH CRUSTY BREAD

Prep Time: 10 Mins

Cook Time: 30 Mins

Resting Time: 18 Hrs

Total Time: 18 Hrs 40 Mins

Serving: 1

Ingredients

- 120 grams all-purpose flour
- 3 grams diamond crystal kosher salt
- 1-gram instant yeast
- 100 grams cool water

Instructions

1. In a bowl, mix the salt, yeast, and flour together.
2. Put the water into the center of the dry ingredients and mix until well mixed. It'll be shaggy and messy. That is okay. Wrap the bowl and set it aside at room temp to rest for twelve to twenty hours (or in the refrigerator for up to 5 days). You want the dough to be double or treble in size, with a flat, bubbly top.
3. During the last hour of the rise time, warm oven to 450°F. Once the oven reaches temperature, set a covered Dutch oven inside and warm to 450°F for thirty minutes. Shape a piece of parchment paper into a ball. Flatten it out, crumple it, then flatten it again.
4. While the Dutch oven preheats, coat a clear countertop with flour. Release the dough from the bowl's sides and place it on the counter. Put a little flour on top, just enough so your hands don't stick.
5. Stretch the dough gently to form a loose square. Take off any extra flour from the top. To roll the flour into a round shape, press the edges together on top and fold the corners of the dough up and across itself. Flip the loaf over so that the seam side is beneath. Cup your hands around it and gently raise and twist the ball of dough against the counter, tucking it inside itself to generate surface tension on top.
6. Lift the dough ball onto the flattened piece of folded parchment paper with the bench scraper. Dust the dough's surface lightly with flour, cover with a dry dish towel, and set aside until the Dutch oven has finished preheating.

7. Gently take the Dutch oven from the oven. Take off the lid and set aside. Cut slits in the top of the loaf to let the steam escape. Gather the corners of the parchment paper, take up the dough, and set it in the Dutch oven. Put the Dutch oven's cover back on.
8. Bake with the lid on for twenty minutes (don't peek!), then remove it and bake for an additional ten minutes or until the top is deep golden brown.
9. Move the fully baked loaf to a cooling rack and let it cool thoroughly prior to slicing.

16. SMALL BATCH BUTTERMILK BISCUITS

Prep Time: 10 Mins

Cook Time: 15 Mins

Total Time: 25 Mins

Serving: 24

Ingredients

- 1 cup of all-purpose flour
- 1½ tsp baking powder
- ⅛ tsp baking soda
- 1 tsp sugar
- ½ tsp kosher salt
- 4 tbsp unsalted butter (very cold & cut into small cubes)
- ⅓ cup of very cold buttermilk

Egg Wash

- 1 large egg
- 1 tbsp water

Instructions

1. Use parchment paper to line a small sheet pan or grease a small cast-iron pan.
2. Mixing (cutting) in butter
3. Toss cold butter cubes into the dried ingredients and, with a pastry cutter or your fingers, combine in the cold butter until you have a combination of flat chunks and crumbly, pea-sized parts of butter in the flour.

Making Biscuits

4. Make a well in the middle of the combination and add the cold buttermilk. Set the wet and dry ingredients together with a sturdy wooden spoon until you have a loose, fairly uniform dough. It's okay that the flour won't look like it's completely mixed in. It will all come together.
5. On a thoroughly floured surface, dump the dough. Use your hands to gently pull everything together into a rough square.
6. Cut the dough into four smaller squares with a bench scraper or knife. On top of each other, stack the dough pieces. Smush it all back into a square. Repeat the cutting and stacking procedure one more time for a total of two cuts and stacks.
7. Roll or pat the dough into a big rectangle approximately ½ inch thick.

Round Biscuits

8. Cut out your biscuits with a biscuit or cookie cutter. Once cutting them out, don't twist the cutter. This will effectively seal the edges of the biscuits, preventing them from completely rising. Simply push straight down and pull straight up. As you go, gather your scraps, shape them again, and cut as many biscuits as you can. You should get about five to six biscuits.

Square Biscuits

9. Cut your dough into four biscuits using a knife or bench scraper.

Baking Instructions

10. Put in the freezer while you warm the oven to 450° F.
11. Massage the tops of the biscuits gently with an egg wash prepared from 1 egg whisked with 1 tbsp water. If desired, sprinkle with flaky salt.
12. Bake in the oven at 450° Fahrenheit for fourteen to sixteen minutes or until golden brown.

17. GARLIC PARMESAN PULL-APART BREAD (SMALL BATCH)

Prep Time: 10 Mins

Cook Time: 23 Mins

Total Time: 33 Mins

Serving: 4

Ingredients

- 1 (7.5 Ounces) tin refrigerated biscuits
- ¼ cup of melted butter
- 1 tsp grated parmesan cheese
- 1 fat garlic clove (peeled and finely minced)
- ¾ tsp dried Italian seasoning
- 3 tbsp grated parmesan cheese to finish

Instructions

1. Set the oven temp to 350°F (180°C), or gas mark 4. Butter a 9 by 4-inch loaf tin and line with baking paper, allowing an overhang on two sides.
2. In a bowl, whisk together the Italian seasoning, butter, garlic, and Parmesan cheese.
3. Open the biscuits. Separate each biscuit and slice it into thirds. Drop several at a time into the butter combination, turning to coat them and then set them in the prepared pan. Continue until all of the biscuits have been coated and arranged in the pan. It is OK for some of them to overlap. (You really do not want any gaps.)
4. Bake for twenty minutes. Continue to the oven for a few more minutes to allow the remaining cheese to melt, then sprinkle it on top.
5. Serve warm. This is great on its own or with a Marinara sauce for dipping.

18. EASY DROP BISCUITS

Prep Time: 10 Mins

Cook Time: 10 Mins

Total Time: 20 Mins

Serving: 10

Ingredients

- 8 tbsp unsalted butter
- 2 cups of all-purpose flour
- 2 tbsp granulated sugar
- 2 tsp baking powder
- 1 tsp table salt
- ½ tsp baking soda
- 1 cup of buttermilk

Instructions

1. Put a rack in the center of your oven and warm it up to 450F (230C).
2. Put parchment paper on a cooking sheet or bake the biscuits straight on a baking sheet that hasn't been greased.
3. Cut the butter into eight pieces and put in a microwave-safe bowl. Warm at 15-second intervals, stirring in between, until melted. To let it cool, set aside.
4. In a big bowl, combine baking powder, baking soda, flour, sugar, and salt; stir to combine well.
5. Put the buttermilk into a large measuring cup or medium-sized bowl. While whisking, gently drizzle in the melted butter until combined (it's okay if it separates slightly).
6. Put the buttermilk combination into the flour combination and fold slowly with a spatula or spoon until just combined. Do not overmix; otherwise, the biscuits will be thick and dry.
7. Scoop batter with approximately three tbsp-sized scoops and put on the prepared baking sheet, spacing biscuits at least 2" apart.
8. Move to a 450F (230C) oven and bake for ten to eleven minutes, or until the tops of the biscuits turn a light golden brown.
9. Take from the oven and let cool on the baking sheet for a few minutes prior to serving. While the biscuits are still warm, brush them with more melted butter if desired.

19. SIMPLE & CLASSIC SHORTBREAD

Total Time: 45 Mins

Serving: 18

Ingredients

- 1 cup of unsalted butter, room temperature
- 1 tsp kosher salt
- ⅔ cup of granulated sugar
- 1.5 tsp vanilla (optional)
- 2 cups of all-purpose flour
- superfine sugar, sparkling sugar, or granulated sugar for sprinkling (optional)

Instructions

1. Warm the oven to 325ºF. You can melt two tbsp of butter if it's not very soft. Put the remainder in a large bowl. Put the melted butter into the bowl; then whisk with a wooden spoon to mix or until the butter is the texture of mayonnaise. Stir in the salt until well combined. If using, add the sugar and vanilla and whisk again to combine. Finally, put the flour and stir just until it's absorbed; the dough will still be lumpy.
2. Press the dough onto an 8- or 9-inch square baking pan that has been ungreased (or coated with parchment paper for ease of removal). In thirty-five to forty minutes for a 9-inch pan and forty-five to fifty minutes for an 8-inch pan, bake until golden brown. Move to a wire rack and let cool. While still warm, cut into squares, bars, or wedges. If desired, distribute with a tbsp or two of sparkling, superfine, or granulated sugar.

20. GRANNY'S MONKEY BREAD RECIPE

Prep Time: 15 Mins

Cook Time: 30 Mins

Total Time: 45 Mins

Serving: 12

Ingredients

- 24 ounces refrigerated biscuit dough
- 1 cup of granulated sugar
- 2 tsp cinnamon
- 1 cup of salted or unsalted butter
- ½ cup of packed golden brown sugar

Instructions

1. **Prepare the pan:** Grease a Bundt or fluted tube pan with butter (12-cup capacity). Warm the oven to 350°F.
2. **Prepare the biscuit pieces:** Separate the biscuits and cut them into four equal bite-size pieces. In a bowl, mix cinnamon and granulated sugar. Drop and roll each piece of dough in the sugar-cinnamon combination to ensure it is well covered. Slowly put the cinnamon-sugar biscuit pieces in the prepared pan.
3. **Create the syrup:** Combine brown sugar and butter in a small saucepan. Add ½ cup of the remaining sugar-cinnamon combination (discard or use in another recipe). Slowly warm the combination until the butter melts and the combination just begins to boil. Take immediately from the flame. Whisk until the sugars are completely dissolved. Do not overcook the syrup; the goal is to help the sugar dissolve. Carefully sprinkle the heated mixture over the rolled dough balls in the pan.
4. **Bake to perfection:** Place the pan in the middle of the heated oven and bake for approximately thirty minutes. Keep an eye on it since baking times might vary.
5. **Let it Rest:** Let the pan rest for approximately five minutes.
6. **Invert and Serve:** Wrap the pan with a big plate and invert to release the monkey bread. To eat, use your fingers to pull off the amount you want (like a monkey would!) and enjoy the sticky, sweet, and bad treat.

(MUFFINS AND CUPCAKES RECIPES)

21. CHOCOLATE CHIP MUFFINS

Prep Time: 20 Mins

Cook Time: 18 Mins

Total Time: 38 Mins

Serving: 6

Ingredients

- 175 grams plain flour or all-purpose flour
- 100 grams caster sugar or granulated sugar
- 2 tsp baking powder
- ¼ tsp salt
- 60 grams unsalted melted butter
- 1 tsp vanilla extract
- 1 large egg
- 80 ml buttermilk
- 75 grams chocolate chips

Instructions

1. Warm the oven to 200 degrees C (390°F) standard/180°C (350°F) fan-forced. Grease six holes in a 6- or 12-hole muffin tin with butter or spray gently with oil.
2. In a big mixing bowl, add sugar, flour, baking powder, and salt and whisk briefly.
3. To a small bowl, add vanilla, melted butter, egg, and buttermilk and stir briefly just to break up the egg yolk.
4. Make a well in the center of the dried ingredients and add the wet ingredients. Whisk together very slowly by hand.
5. Add the chocolate chips. After that, fold until the combination is just mixed – be careful not to over it, or your muffins will be tough.
6. Fill the prepared muffin tin with the muffin batter. Bake for five minutes prior to turning down the flame to 180 C (350 F) standard / 160 C (320 F) fan-forced and bake for a further thirteen to fifteen minutes or until muffins are golden brown.

22. SMALL BATCH BLUEBERRY MUFFIN RECIPE

Prep Time: 5 Mins

Cook Time: 15 Mins

Bake Time: 22 Mins

Total Time: 42 Mins

Serving: 4

Ingredients

For the Small Batch Blueberry Muffins

- 1¼ cups of all-purpose flour
- 1 tsp baking powder
- ¼ tsp kosher salt
- ¼ cup of whole milk at room temperature
- ¼ tsp pure vanilla extract
- ½ cup of granulated sugar
- 4 tbsp unsalted butter at room temperature
- 1 large egg at room temperature
- 1¼ cups of fresh blueberries at room temperature

Assembly

- canola or vegetable oil cooking spray
- 4 tsp granulated white sugar

Instructions

For the Small Batch Blueberry Muffins

1. **Make the muffin batter:** Whisk the baking powder, flour, and salt in a medium bowl. In a small liquid measuring cup, mix together the milk and vanilla.
2. In the stand blender bowl fitted with a paddle attachment, mix the sugar and butter. Mix on medium-high for approximately 2 to 3 minutes, scraping down the bowl's bottom and sides as required, until light, fluffy, and doubled in volume. Lower the mixer to low and add the egg.

3. Add the dried ingredients in three equal parts, then the wet ingredients in two parts, while the blender is still on low. Beat until just mixed, then scrape the bottom and sides out of the bowl again, then beat on low for another 30 seconds. Crush half of the blueberries with your hands until they are juicy; add to the mixture and raise the mixer speed to high for about five to ten seconds to encourage the berries to release even more juice. Lower the blender immediately to low and add the rest of the berries, mixing until evenly distributed throughout the batter, another thirty seconds.
4. **Rest the muffin batter:** Wrap the bowl with plastic cover and let the batter to sit at room temperature for one hour.
5. **Prep your oven and pans:** Set a rack in the middle of the oven and warm it to 400°F using the convect setting (if possible) while the batter rests. Spray the inside and border of every other cavity in a muffin tray generously with cooking spray. However, you will only need to prepare four cavities; there is no need to spray the remaining ones! If you're using a regular muffin tin, set it so that the short side faces you, then prepare the center cavity of the top row, the outside two cavities of the second row, and the middle cavity of the third row.
6. Fill each sprayed cavity with six tbsp of the batter with a 1-or 3-tbsp cookie dough scoop. Distribute one tsp of granulated sugar on top of each cavity, aiming for the batter and avoiding the pan. Fill the outer cavities of the muffin tin's final row with warm water at least ⅔ of the way up.
7. **Bake the muffins:** Bake the muffins for twenty-two to twenty-four minutes or until they are domed and golden brown on the edges. A skewer placed into the center of a muffin should emerge with a few crumbs attached. Cool the muffins in the muffin tray on a wire rack for fifteen minutes before running an offset spatula beneath the edges of the blueberry muffin tops to keep them from adhering to the pan. Just drag the offset spatula under the edges—you don't want to cut into the muffin bottom and decapitate it from the top!
8. After unsticking the muffin tops, let the muffins cool fully in the pans until room temperature. Do not turn out the muffins while they are still warm. Because these muffins are so top-heavy, you could accidentally rip the tops and bottoms apart if the cake is still warm! Before taking them out of the pan, wait until they are totally cool. To flip each muffin out of the pan and raise it from its base, run the offset spatula underneath the top of each muffin once more and tilt it gently upward.
9. **Serve and store:** Serve heated or at room temperature. The muffins are best on the day they are made, but can be individually wrapped in plastic and refrigerated at room temperature for up to two days.

23. CHOCOLATE CREAM CHEESE MUFFINS

Prep Time: 5 Mins

Cook Time: 15 Mins

Bake Time: 22 Mins

Total Time: 42 Mins

Serving: 4

Ingredients

- 135 g all-purpose flour
- 110 g granulated sugar
- 35 g Dutch process cocoa
- 1 tsp baking powder
- ½ tsp baking soda
- 1 tsp espresso powder
- ¾ tsp kosher salt
- 100 g Greek yoghurt or sour cream at room temperature
- 75 g whole milk at room temperature
- 70 g melted and cooled unsalted butter
- 30 g neutral oil
- 1 egg at room temperature
- 110 g coarsely chopped dark chocolate plus extra for the tops
- 100 g full-fat cream cheese at room temp

Instructions

1. Set oven temperature to 400°F, or 205°C. Grease and line a 6-hole muffin tray with paper liners (optional: cut a sheet of parchment into a 5 ½" square and push it into each cavity). Alternatively, use a twelve-hole muffin tray and fill every second cavity, allowing space between them to bake more evenly.
2. In a medium bowl, stir the baking powder, flour, sugar, cocoa, baking soda, espresso powder, and salt.
3. Whisk together the yogurt, milk, melted butter, oil, and egg in a second bowl. With a spatula, put the wet ingredients to the dried and fold just until mixed. Mix in the chocolate until combined.

4. Scoop approximately two tbsp of batter into each muffin cavity. Split the cream cheese into six about equal pieces and gently push them into the batter of each muffin. To top the cream cheese, split the remaining batter amongst the muffins. To cover the cream cheese, softly spread it with a spoon or spatula. If desired, distribute some dark chocolate over the tops of the muffins.
5. Bake the muffins for approximately twenty minutes or until the top springs back when lightly pressed. Do not overbake since they will dry out.
6. Take it from the oven and let it cool in the pan for five to ten minutes prior to moving it to a wire rack to cool fully.

24. SMALL BATCH VANILLA CUPCAKES

Prep Time: 15 Mins

Cook Time: 15 Mins

Total Time: 30 Mins

Servings: 5

Ingredients

Cupcakes

- ½ cup of all-purpose flour
- ½ tsp baking powder
- ⅛ tsp salt
- 1 large egg
- ¼ cup of granulated sugar
- 2 tsp pure vanilla extract
- 4 tbsp unsalted butter (melted & slightly cooled)
- ¼ cup of milk (preferably whole or 2% milk)

Vanilla Frosting

- 5 tbsp unsalted butter at room temperature
- 1¼ cups of powdered sugar + more if needed
- ¼ tsp pure vanilla extract
- 1 tsp milk plus more if needed

Instructions

Cupcakes

1. Warm the oven to 350° F. In a muffin pan, put five liners.
2. In a small mixing bowl, mix baking powder, flour, and salt. Set aside.
3. In a big bowl, whisk the egg and sugar for about thirty seconds. Combine the melted butter and vanilla extract by mixing them in completely with a whisk.
4. Whisk half of the dry ingredients and half of the wet ingredients together until well combined. Add the milk and stir until it's just mixed. Add the remaining dried ingredients and stir until mixed (being careful not to overmix).
5. Split the batter evenly between five muffin cups (each cup will be between ⅔ and ¾ full). Bake for fourteen to sixteen minutes, or until a piece of toothpick introduced into the middle of the cupcake comes out clean. Let it cool thoroughly prior to frosting.

Frosting

6. Combine powdered sugar and butter and beat until smooth. Combine one tsp of milk with vanilla extract. Mix for several minutes at medium speed or until light and fluffy. If the frosting seems too thick, add a little milk; if it appears too thin, add a bit more powdered sugar.
7. To frost the cupcakes, use a piping bag and an open-star pastry tip. If desired, add sprinkles on top.

25. SMALL-BATCH CHOCOLATE CHIP MUFFINS

Total Time: 30 Mins

Servings: 6

Ingredients

- 1 cup of flour
- ⅓ cup of sugar + more for sprinkling on top
- 1 tsp baking powder
- ¼ tsp salt
- ⅓ cup of buttermilk
- 3 tbsp melted butter
- ½ tsp vanilla extract
- 1 egg

- ½ cup of mini chocolate chips plus additional for sprinkling on top

Instructions

1. Whisk the baking powder, flour, sugar, and salt together in a medium bowl. Whisk the egg, buttermilk, melted butter, and vanilla extract in a small bowl. Put the wet ingredients into the dry.
2. Stir together for a few turns. Toss in your micro chocolate chips while the combination still has pockets of dry flour in it. Keep to whisk until no dry pockets remain, but don't over-mix.
3. Cover the batter and set it aside for thirty minutes on your counter. It will help everything stick together before baking, and it will also help you get muffins with high tops.
4. Warm the oven to 400 degrees. Sprinkle baking spray on your baking pan. You want the spray to cover mostly the top of the pan so that the overhang doesn't stick. Put paper cups on the line.
5. When your batter has rested for a full thirty minutes, scoop evenly into your prepared pan. Now, the muffin cups should be very full, with batter almost reaching the top of the cups. You should have six muffins. Distribute the tops generously with extra sugar and tiny chips.
6. Bake for sixteen to twenty minutes, or until the muffins are puffed and lightly golden brown, with only a few crumbs on the toothpick. When removed from the oven, use a butter knife to keep any overhanging parts from sticking to the pan. Cool the muffins fully in the pan, and enjoy!

26. SMALL BATCH ONE BANANA MUFFINS

Total Time: 30 Mins

Servings: 6

Ingredients

- 1 cup of all-purpose flour
- ½ tsp baking powder
- ½ tsp baking soda
- ½ tsp cinnamon
- ¼ tsp salt
- ¼ cup of unsalted melted butter
- 1 overripe banana (will equal about ½ cup of mashed banana)
- ⅓ cup of packed brown sugar

- 1 large egg
- ½ tsp vanilla extract
- ½ cup of dark or semisweet chocolate chips (optional)
- 1 tbsp turbinado sugar (optional for sprinkling on top)

Instructions

1. Set the oven temp to 425 degrees F (218°C). Line or grease every other cup of a twelve-cup muffin tray (the recipe yields six muffins; using every other cup allows for greater airflow and taller muffins).
2. In a medium bowl, stir dry ingredients: flour, cinnamon, baking soda, baking powder, and salt. Set aside.
3. Melt the butter in a big, microwave-safe bowl. Add banana and mash completely with a stir or fork. Stir in the egg, brown sugar, and vanilla extract until well combined.
4. In the bowl containing the wet ingredients, add the dried ingredients and stir until a batter forms. Stir until just combined; don't overmix. If you are using chocolate chips or other add-ins, fold them in last.
5. **Optional:** Allow batter to sit at room temperature for fifteen to twenty-five minutes prior to scooping for the tallest muffins.
6. Spoon the batter equally into the six muffin cups. Top with a liberal dusting of turbinado or granulated sugar and, if preferred, more chocolate chips.
7. Bake for five minutes at 425° Fahrenheit (218°C), then reduce to 350 degrees F (180 degrees C) without opening the oven door and bake for another twelve to fifteen minutes until domed and set. A toothpick put into the center should come out clean, with just a few crumbs attached.
8. Allow to cool for a few minutes, then enjoy!

Notes

1. **Storage:** Baked muffins are kept well covered at room temp for 1-2 days or refrigerated for up to 1 week.

27. MOIST SMALL BATCH LEMON BLUEBERRY MUFFINS

Prep Time: 10 Mins

Cook Time: 20 Mins

Total Time: 30 Mins

Servings: 6-8

Ingredients

- 1 tbsp lemon zest
- 125 g granulated sugar
- 1 large egg
- 120 g sour cream
- 60 g canola oil
- 30 g lemon juice
- 155 g divided all-purpose flour
- 2 tsp baking powder
- ¼ tsp baking soda
- ¼ tsp fine sea salt
- 155 g blueberries

Instructions

1. Set oven temperature to 400°F, or 205°C. Sprinkle a 6-cup muffin pan with nonstick spray or line it with cupcake liners, and put it aside.
2. In a big bowl, combine the granulated sugar and lemon zest. Using your fingers, rub the sugar until it is well combined, fragrant, and yellow.
3. Add the egg and stir until the combination has thickened and is light in color, approximately two to three minutes. Stir in the sour cream, oil, and lemon juice until thoroughly mixed and no sour cream lumps remain, about 1 to 2 minutes. Set aside.
4. Stir and add 1 cup of flour, baking powder, baking soda, and salt until it is mostly mixed. Whisk the blueberries in the remaining ¼ cup of flour, then combine with the batter. Carefully fold everything together until it's all just mixed.
5. Fill every muffin pan cup all the way to the top with batter; each cup needs 4½ tbsp of batter. If desired, distribute the tops with granulated sugar.
6. Bake the muffins for approximately fifteen to seventeen minutes, or until the tip of a toothpick introduced in the center comes out mostly clean. Let the muffins to chill in the pan for ten minutes prior to removing to a wire rack to cool completely.

28. PLAIN MUFFIN RECIPE

Prep Time: 5 Mins

Cook Time: 18 Mins

Total Time: 23 Mins

Servings: 6

Ingredients

- 1 cup of all-purpose flour
- ¼ cup of granulated sugar
- 1½ tsp baking powder
- ¼ tsp salt
- 1 beaten egg
- ¼ cup of oil
- ¼ cup of milk

Instructions

1. Warm the oven to 400 degrees F.
2. Line a muffin tray with six muffin liners and use the middle holes.
3. Whisk together the baking powder, flour, sugar, and salt in a medium bowl.
4. To the dry ingredients, add oil, milk, and egg.
5. Whisk until just incorporated; do not overmix.
6. Bake the muffins, scooped into the prepared tin, for fifteen to eighteen minutes.

29. SMALL BATCH CARROT CAKE

Prep Time: 20 Mins

Cook Time: 25 Mins

Total Time: 45 Mins

Servings: 4

Ingredients

- ½ cup of all-purpose flour
- ½ tsp nutmeg
- 1 tsp cinnamon
- ½ tsp baking soda
- ¼ tsp salt
- ¼ cup of sugar
- ¼ cup of brown sugar
- ¼ cup of canola oil or melted butter
- 1 egg
- ½ tsp vanilla
- ⅔ cup of grated carrot
- ¼ cup of finely chopped walnuts (optional)

Cream Cheese Frosting

- 2 Ounces softened cream cheese
- 3 tbsp softened butter
- ½ tsp vanilla
- 1 cup of powdered sugar
- 1 tsp whipping cream or milk
- ¼ cup of walnuts chopped for garnish on top

Instructions

1. Flour and grease 6-inch cake pan. Use wax or parchment paper to line the bottom.
2. Warm the oven to 350 degrees F.
3. Mix flour, nutmeg, cinnamon, baking soda, and salt in a small bowl.
4. In another bowl, combine the sugars, oil, vanilla, and egg. Add the flour combination and whisk to combine.
5. Fold in the grated carrots.
6. Put the batter into the prepared pan.

7. Bake for thirty to thirty-five minutes or until a toothpick comes out clean.
8. Let the cake cool in the pan on a cooling rack. Remove and frost.

Cream Cheese Frosting

9. To achieve a creamy consistency, combine the cream cheese and butter in a blender.
10. Add in whipping cream, sugar, and vanilla and combine until mixed and fluffy.
11. Frost either the top or the entire cake.
12. Distribute with chopped walnuts.

Notes

1. Store leftover carrot cake in the refrigerator.
2. The cake can sit at room temp prior to serving to warm up.
3. Carrot cake can stay in the refrigerator for approximately one week and may be frozen for two to three months.

30. MINI POUND CAKE

Prep Time: 10 Mins

Cook Time: 45 Mins

Cool Time: 10 Mins

Total Time: 1 Hr 5 Mins

Servings: 4

Ingredients

- ¼ cup of softened salted butter plus 1 tbsp more for greasing
- ¾ cup of granulated sugar
- 1 large egg
- ½ tsp lemon juice
- ¼ tsp vanilla extract
- ¾ cup of all-purpose flour
- ⅛ tsp baking powder
- ⅛ tsp salt
- ¼ cup of low-fat milk

Instructions

1. Preheat the oven to 350° Fahrenheit (177 degrees Celsius).
2. In a 5x5-inch or 4x6-inch baking dish, lightly butter it. Put the baking dish on top of a baking sheet.
3. In a small bowl, blend butter and sugar with an electric blender until well-mixed.
4. Beat in the egg, lemon juice, and vanilla.
5. Stir the baking powder, flour, and salt in a separate small bowl. Add to the sugar and butter combination and combine.
6. Whisk in the milk.
7. Put the batter into the prepared cooking dish and bake for forty to forty-five minutes or until golden.
8. Let to cool for ten minutes prior to inverting over a platter.
9. Best if served warm.

31. BANANA CHOCOLATE CHIP MUFFINS WITH STREUSEL

Prep Time: 10 Mins

Cook Time: 20 Mins

Cool Time: 30 Mins

Total Time: 1 Hr

Servings: 7

Ingredients

For the Streusel

- ⅓ cup of all-purpose flour
- 3 tbsp packed light brown sugar
- ½ tsp nutmeg
- 2 tbsp unsalted butter (room temperature & sliced into four pieces)

For the Muffins

- 5 tbsp unsalted melted butter
- 2 medium ripe bananas (peeled and coarsely mashed)
- ½ cup of granulated sugar
- 1 large egg (room temperature)
- 1 tbsp real vanilla extract

- ½ tsp cinnamon
- ½ tsp ground nutmeg
- ½ tsp baking powder
- ½ tsp baking soda
- ½ tsp sea salt
- 1 cup + 2 tbsp all-purpose flour
- ⅓ cup + 1 tbsp water room temperature
- ⅓ cup of mini dark chocolate chips (+ extra to sprinkle over the tops)

Instructions

For the Streusel

1. Stir the nutmeg, brown sugar, and flour in a medium-sized bowl. Use a pastry blender, your fingertips, or a fork to combine the butter until it resembles wet sand and forms clumps when pressed. Put it in the fridge to get cold. If storing it for longer than thirty minutes, keep it in a covered container.

For the Muffins

2. To a big mixing bowl, add the melted butter, nutmeg, baking powder, mashed bananas, sugar, egg, vanilla, cinnamon, baking soda, and salt and stir until completely blended about 1 minute. Alternately, add the flour and water in two batches, beginning with the flour and ending with the water. Fold in the chocolate chips, put the bowl aside, and allow the batter to rest while you warm the oven (ideally, let the batter rest for ten to twenty minutes; this is optional!).
3. Warm the oven to 375 degrees Fahrenheit (190°C), and line every other muffin well with a muffin liner. Fill each muffin liner with almost completely covered muffin batter. Evenly sprinkle the streusel between the seven muffins and top with mini chocolate chips. Bake in the middle of the oven for approximately eighteen to twenty minutes or until they bounce back when lightly pressed in the center. Let to cool in the muffin tray for about ten minutes, then use a butter knife to remove them and finish cooling on a rack. Enjoy!

32. SMALL BATCH BANANA MUFFINS

Prep Time: 10 Mins

Cook Time: 20 Mins

Total Time: 30 Mins

Servings: 6

Ingredients

- ½ cup of sugar
- 2 divided overripe bananas
- 6 tbsp salted melted butter
- 1 large egg
- ½ tsp vanilla extract
- 1 cup of all-purpose flour
- 1 tsp baking soda
- ¼ tsp salt

Instructions

1. Preheat the oven to 350° Fahrenheit (177 degrees C).
2. Spray or butter the muffin tin a little.
3. In a big bowl, whip the sugar and one of the bananas together until well blended.
4. Add the egg, cooled melted butter, and vanilla, and beat thoroughly.
5. Mix the baking soda, flour, and salt until just combined.
6. Use a fork to peel and mash the remaining banana on a small plate. Fold it into the batter.
7. Fill up the muffin tins ¾ of the way to the top with batter.
8. Bake for twenty to twenty-five or until a toothpick introduced into the muffin comes out clean.

33. HOMEMADE BLUEBERRY MUFFIN RECIPE

Prep Time: 5 Mins

Cook Time: 20 Mins

Total Time: 25 Mins

Servings: 12

Ingredients

- 1½ cups of all-purpose flour
- ¾ cup of granulated sugar plus one tbsp for muffin tops
- ½ tsp salt
- 2 tsp baking powder
- ⅓ cup of vegetable oil
- 1 large egg
- ⅓-½ cup of milk
- 1 ½ tsp vanilla extract
- 6-8 ounces fresh or frozen blueberries

Instructions

1. Warm the oven to 400°F.
2. In a big bowl, stir flour, sugar, baking powder, and salt,
3. Use a measuring cup with a capacity of at least one cup and add vegetable oil, egg, and milk until the cup is full.
4. Stir in the vanilla until well-mixed.
5. Combine the milk combination with the flour and sugar in a bowl and blend with a fork. Don't overmix. (The muffin batter will be rather thick.
6. Put blueberries and gently fold them into the muffin batter with a spatula or spoon.
7. Split the batter between the muffin cups, filling about ½ full.
8. Distribute a little sugar on top of each muffin.
9. Bake for approximately fifteen to twenty minutes.

34. BASIC MUFFIN RECIPE

Prep Time: 20 Mins

Cook Time: 25 Mins

Total Time: 45 Mins

Servings: 20

Ingredients

- 2 medium eggs
- 125 ml vegetable oil
- 250 ml semi-skimmed milk
- 250 g golden caster sugar
- 400 g self-raising flour
- 1 tsp salt
- 100 g chocolate chips (optional)

Instructions

1. Warm the oven to 200 °C/180 °C fan/gas. 6. Line two muffin tins with paper cases. In a big bowl, beat two medium eggs lightly with a handheld electric blender for one minute.
2. Mix in 125ml vegetable oil and 250ml semi-skimmed milk until just combined, then add 250g golden caster sugar and whisk to make a smooth batter.
3. Sift in 400g self-raising flour and one tsp salt (or 400g plain flour and three tsp baking powder, if using), and combine just until smooth. To avoid making tough muffins, be careful not to mix the batter too much.
4. If using, whisk in 100g of chocolate chips or dried fruit.
5. Bake muffin cases until two-thirds full, risen, and firm to the touch or until a skewer introduced into the center comes out clean, approximately twenty to twenty-five minutes. If the trays do not fit on one shelf, swap the shelves after fifteen minutes of cooking.
6. Let the muffins to cool in the tin for a few minutes, then move to a wire rack to chill completely.

35. COFFEE CAKE MUFFINS

Prep Time: 15 Mins

Cook Time: 20 Mins

Total Time: 35 Mins

Servings: 4

Ingredients

For the Crumb Topping

- ¼ cup of lightly packed brown sugar
- 1 tbsp granulated sugar
- pinch of salt
- ¼ tsp ground cinnamon
- 1 tbsp unsalted melted butter
- 3 tbsp all-purpose flour

For the Muffins

- ¼ cup of canola oil
- ⅓ cup of granulated sugar
- pinch of salt
- 1 large egg
- 2 tbsp heavy cream
- ½ tsp vanilla extract
- ⅓ cup + 1 tbsp all-purpose flour
- ⅛ tsp baking soda
- ⅛ tsp baking powder
- ¼ tsp ground cinnamon
- ⅛ tsp ground nutmeg

Instructions

1. Warm the oven to 375° Fahrenheit and line a muffin pan with four cups of cupcake liners.
2. In a small bowl, combine all of the crumb topping ingredients and pinch together to form crumbs. Set aside.

3. Next, use an electric mixer on medium speed to beat the oil and sugar in a medium bowl for five minutes. Then, add the salt, egg, cream, and vanilla and beat for fifteen seconds.
4. Distribute the remaining dry ingredients on top, then beat just until combined.
5. Scoop 1½ tbsp batter into each muffin cup. Top with a spoonful of crumb topping, and then split the rest of the batter between all muffin cups. Top the muffins with the remaining streusel.
6. Put it in the oven and bake for nineteen to twenty-three minutes, or until an inserted toothpick comes out fresh and the topping is nice and golden brown.

36. HEALTHIER CHOCOLATE CHIP MUFFIN

Prep Time: 5 Mins

Cook Time: 17 Mins

Total Time: 30 Mins

Servings: 1

Ingredients

- 3 tbsp white whole wheat flour (spooned & leveled)
- ¼ tsp baking powder
- dash of salt
- 1 and ½ tbsp semi-sweet chocolate chips
- ½ tsp pure vanilla extract
- 1 tbsp unsalted melted butter or coconut oil
- 1 tbsp + 1 tsp milk
- 1 tbsp granulated sugar

Instructions

1. Set oven temperature to 350°F (177°C). Line the muffin tin with one-liner. Set aside.
2. In a small bowl, combine baking powder, flour, salt, and chocolate chips together. Combine the vanilla, melted butter, milk, and sugar. Combine everything until it's just mixed. DO NOT over-mix.
3. Put the batter into the prepared muffin liner. Bake for seventeen minutes or until a toothpick inserted in the middle comes out clean.

37. BEST EVER MUFFINS

Prep Time: 10 Mins

Cook Time: 25 Mins

Total Time: 35 Mins

Servings: 12

Ingredients

- 2 cups of all-purpose flour
- 3 tsp baking powder
- ½ tsp salt
- ¾ cup of white sugar
- 1 egg
- 1 cup of milk
- ¼ cup of vegetable oil

Directions

1. Set the oven's temperature to 400°F or 200°C. Grease a 12-cup muffin tray or line the cups with paper liners.
2. In a big bowl, whisk together baking powder, flour, sugar, and salt; make a well in the center.
3. In a small bowl, mix the egg with a fork, then whisk in the milk and oil. Put the egg combination into the flour mixture all at once, and use a fork to mix quickly and lightly until just moist. It will be a lumpy batter. Fill up each muffin cup ¾ of the way to the top with batter.
4. Bake in the heated oven until the tops spring back when lightly pressed, approximately twenty-five minutes.

38. ULTIMATE MUFFINS RECIPE

Prep Time: 10 Mins

Cook Time: 30 Mins

Total Time: 40 Mins

Servings: 12

Ingredients

- 2 ¼ cups of all-purpose flour
- ½ cup of granulated sugar
- ¼ cup of brown sugar
- ½ tsp fine salt
- 1 tbsp baking powder
- 1 cup of buttermilk at room temperature
- 1 stick melted and cooled unsalted butter
- 2 large eggs at room temperature
- 1 tsp vanilla extract (if desired)
- add-ins and flavorings of your choice
- coarse sugar for sprinkling (if desired)

Directions

1. Warm the oven to 400 °F. In the upper third of the oven, put a rack. Use paper liners to line a standard muffin tin.
2. Stir together the salt, flour, sugar, and baking powder in a large bowl.
3. Beat the butter, egg, vanilla, and buttermilk together in a liquid measuring cup. Put into the dry ingredients and whisk until a few streaks of flour remain. Whisk in any desired add-ins, like fruit or chips.
4. Cover the muffin batter and put it in the fridge for an hour or overnight if you have time. This will result in more moist, soft, and tall muffins.
5. In the muffin tin cups, split evenly. If desired, sprinkle each with coarse sugar.
6. Bake until golden brown, and a toothpick introduced in the middle comes out clean, for about 16 to 18 minutes.

39. PUMPKIN GINGERBREAD MUFFINS

Prep Time: 5 Mins

Total Time: 25 Mins

Servings: 12

Ingredients

- 4 tbsp melted butter
- ½ cup of brown sugar
- 2 eggs
- 1 tsp vanilla
- ¼ cup of molasses
- ⅔ cup of pumpkin puree
- 1.5 cups of white whole wheat flour
- 1 tsp baking soda
- ½ tsp baking powder
- 1 tsp cinnamon
- 1 tsp ground ginger (more if desired)

Instructions

1. In a large bowl, combine first six ingredients; whisk until well combined.
2. Stir in remaining ingredients until just combined.
3. Scoop into greased or lined muffin tins.
4. Bake at 375 degrees for twenty to twenty-two minutes.

40. CINNAMON MUFFINS

Prep Time: 15 Mins

Cook Time: 25 Mins

Total Time: 40 Mins

Servings: 12

Ingredients

For the Cinnamon Sugar Topping

- 3 tbsp packed brown sugar (dark or light)
- 1 ½ tsp cinnamon (see note 1)

For the Muffin Batter

- 2 cups of all-purpose flour
- 2 tsp baking powder
- ½ tsp salt
- ½ tsp cinnamon
- pinch nutmeg
- ½ cup of granulated sugar
- ⅓ cup of packed brown sugar (dark or light)
- 2 large eggs
- ⅔ cup of neutral oil (vegetable, canola, etc.)
- 1 cup of milk
- 1 tsp vanilla

Instructions

1. Set the oven's temperature to 350°F, or 177°C.
2. Put cupcake liners in the cups of a 12-cup muffin tray, or oil the tin thoroughly with nonstick cooking spray. Set aside.
3. To prepare the cinnamon sugar topping, combine three tbsp packed brown sugar with 1 ½ tsp cinnamon in a small bowl. Set aside.
4. In a medium bowl, stir the salt, flour, baking powder, ½ tsp cinnamon, and pinch of nutmeg. Set aside.
5. In a large separate bowl, put the brown sugar for the batter. If the brown sugar contains any lumps, use your fingers or a fork to break them apart. Then, combine the granulated sugar, eggs, oil, milk, and vanilla. Stir together until well combined.

6. In a few batches, combine the dry ingredients with the wet ingredients, whisking gently between each addition. Whisk just until mixed (a few lumps are acceptable; do not overmix).
7. Fill each muffin tin approximately ⅓ full with batter. Then, distribute about ½ tsp of the cinnamon sugar combination equally over each layer of batter. Then, use the remaining batter to top each muffin. Distribute the rest of the cinnamon sugar combination evenly on top of each muffin.
8. Bake in the heated oven for twenty-two to twenty-six minutes, or until the top of the muffin is firm and a toothpick introduced in the middle comes out clean (a couple of crumbs are ok, but no wet batter).
9. Let the muffins chill in the tin for approximately ten minutes, then take to a wire rack to continue cooling.

Notes

1. To add more cinnamon flavor to the cinnamon sugar topping, increase the quantity from 1 ½ to 2 tsp!

(COOKIES, BROWINIES AND BARS RECIPES)

41. SMALL-BATCH SUGAR COOKIES

Prep Time: 10 Mins

Cook Time: 10 Mins

Cool Time: 15 Mins

Total Time: 35 Mins

Servings: 6

Ingredients
Small-Batch Sugar Cookies

- ⅓ cup of salted softened butter
- ⅓ cup + 1 tbsp granulated sugar
- 1 large egg yolk
- ½ tsp vanilla extract or ⅛ tsp almond extract
- ¾ cup + 1 tbsp all-purpose flour
- ¼ tsp baking soda
- ⅛ tsp salt
- ⅓ cup of granulated sugar, powdered sugar, or sprinkles for rolling (optional)

Optional Glaze

- 1 cup of sifted powdered sugar
- 1 tbsp milk + more to reach desired consistency
- ¼ tsp vanilla extract
- 2 tsp light corn syrup
- 2-4 tsp food coloring (optional)

Instructions
Small-Batch Sugar Cookies

1. Warm the oven to 350°F and prepare a cooking sheet with parchment paper.
2. In a medium bowl, cream gently the butter and sugar until light and fluffy.
3. Put the egg yolk and vanilla and beat until well mixed.

4. Combine the salt, baking soda, and flour until the dough begins to aggregate and there is no dried flour remaining at the bottom of the bowl.
5. Split the dough into six pieces and form into balls. If rolling in distributes or sugar, do so now.
6. Put the dough on the cookie sheet, evenly spaced, and use your palm to press the cookies to ½-inch thickness.
7. Put the cookies in the oven for nine to twelve minutes or until the bottom edges turn a light brown color. Cool fully on the cookie sheet.

Optional Glaze

8. Combine the vanilla, powdered sugar, and milk in a medium bowl when the cookies have cooled. Whisk until completely blended.
9. Add corn syrup and whisk until smooth. Stir in two to four droplets of food coloring, if desirable, until the color is consistent. To get a drizzling consistency, add extra milk if needed.
10. Spoon the glaze over the cookies and let it set for approximately ten to fifteen minutes. Enjoy!

42. PB&J THUMBPRINT COOKIES

Prep Time: 5 Mins

Cook Time: 10 Mins

Total Time: 15 Mins

Servings: 8

Ingredients

- 1 tbsp coconut oil
- 2 tbsp peanut butter
- 3 tbsp maple syrup
- ½ cup of flour gf all-purpose if desired
- ⅛ tsp baking soda
- ⅛ tsp salt
- raspberry filling
- ¼ cup of fresh or frozen raspberries
- 1 tsp chia seeds

Instructions

1. Warm the oven to 350°F and prepare a cookie sheet with parchment.
2. Microwave your berries for thirty seconds at a time, then mash them and add the chia seeds, stirring until smooth. Set away to set.
3. Warm the coconut oil in a bowl, then stir in the peanut butter & maple syrup until well combined.
4. Add flour, make a slight well in the middle, and add baking soda and salt. Combine the soda with the flour. Whisk to combine and form cookie dough.
5. If the cookie dough is too dried, add a drop of water; if it's too wet, add a pinch of flour.
6. Scoop the dough, roll it between your palms, flatten it carefully, create a thumbprint on each cookie, and bake for ten minutes. You might wish to re-indent them after baking, but first allow them to cool.
7. Let your cookies cool fully and fill their centers with one tsp of filling each. Enjoy!

43. SMALL-BATCH SNICKERDOODLES (THICK AND SOFT)

Prep Time: 5 Mins

Cook Time: 10 Mins

Total Time: 15 Mins

Servings: 12

Ingredients

- 188 g all-purpose flour
- 1 tsp tartar cream
- ½ tsp baking soda
- 1 tsp ground cinnamon
- ¼ tsp salt
- 113 g unsalted butter, room temperature
- 150 g granulated sugar
- 1 tsp vanilla paste or extract
- 1 large egg

Coating

- 50 g granulated sugar
- ½ tsp ground cinnamon

Instructions

1. Set the oven's temperature to 375°F (190°C). Use parchment paper to line a big cookie sheet.
2. In a small bowl, stir together the flour, tartar cream, cinnamon, baking soda, and salt, and set this flour combination aside.
3. In a big mixing bowl, combine the room-temperature butter and granulated sugar and beat for a minute and a half until light and creamy.
4. Blend in the egg and vanilla until thoroughly mixed. Combine the dried and wet ingredients and beat on low speed until you get a thick but slightly sticky cookie dough.
5. To roll, mix the granulated sugar and ground cinnamon in a separate small bowl.
6. To make 12 large cookie dough balls, use a medium cookie scoop or approximately 1 ½ - 2 tbsp per ball.
7. Roll each cookie dough ball in the cinnamon-sugar combination until it is completely covered.
8. Put the cookies at least 3 inches apart on baking sheets lined with parchment paper. Bake for approximately ten minutes, or until the cookies are fluffy and thick, with little crunchy edges. The amount of time it takes to bake is determined on the oven use. Look for the cookies' tops to be extremely soft.
9. If you want to slightly flatten the cookies, hit the tray on the bench once or twice after it comes out of the oven.
10. Let the cookies to chill on the cookie sheet for five minutes prior to moving them to a wire rack to cool even further.

44. DOUBLE CHOCOLATE COOKIES

Prep Time: 10 Mins

Cook Time: 10 Mins

Total Time: 20 Mins

Servings: 10

Ingredients

- ¼ cup of unsalted softened butter
- ½ cup of packed light brown sugar
- 1 tsp pure vanilla extract
- ¼ tsp salt
- 1 large egg yolk
- ¼ tsp baking soda
- ½ cup of all-purpose flour
- 2 tbsp cocoa powder
- ½ cup of dark chocolate

Instructions

1. Warm the oven to 350° F. Use parchment paper to line a large baking sheet.
2. In a small bowl, use a spatula to combine the vanilla, butter, brown sugar, and salt until smooth and creamy. Combine egg yolk and baking soda. To eliminate any lumps, combine flour and cocoa, then fold in. Fold in the chocolate.
3. Roll heaping tbsp of dough into balls and set on the prepared cooking sheet, spacing them about two inches apart. Slightly flatten. Bake for about eight to ten minutes or until puffed and set around the edges but still tender in the center. Move to a wire rack to chill completely, but eat a few while they're still warm!

45. PEANUT BUTTER COOKIES RECIPE

Prep Time: 15 Mins

Cook Time: 15 Mins

Total Time: 30 Mins

Servings: 10

Ingredients

- ¼ cup of unsalted softened butter
- ¼ cup of peanut butter
- ¼ cup of packed brown sugar
- 2 tbsp granulated sugar
- 1 large egg yolk
- ¼ tsp vanilla
- 1½ tsp milk
- pinch salt
- ½ tsp baking soda
- ¾ cup + 2 tbsp all-purpose flour

Instructions

1. Warm the oven to 350 degrees Fahrenheit. Line a cooking sheet with parchment or Silpat baking mats.
2. In the electric blender bowl fitted with the paddle attachment, cream butter, peanut butter, and both sugars for approximately two to three minutes. Mix in the baking soda, eggs, vanilla, milk, and salt until thoroughly blended. Gently add flour and stir until the dough comes together.
3. Scoop two tbsp-sized cookie balls onto the prepared sheet, spacing them 2 inches apart. Press the cookies down with a fork in a crisscross pattern.
4. Bake for about ten to fifteen minutes, until the bottoms begin to turn light brown and the cookies are no longer glossy in the center.
5. Keep in an airtight jar for up to three days, or freeze for up to one month.

46. SMALL BATCH ALMOND JOY COOKIES

Prep Time: 20 Mins

Cook Time: 10 Mins

Total Time: 30 Mins

Servings: 24

Ingredients

- 1⅛ cups of all-purpose flour
- ½ tsp baking soda
- ¼ tsp salt
- ½ cup of unsalted softened butter
- ⅓ cup of sugar
- ⅓ cup of brown sugar
- 1 tsp vanilla extract
- 1 egg
- 1½ cups of semi-sweet chocolate chips
- 1 cup of sweetened coconut flakes
- ¾ cup of sliced almonds

Instructions

1. Warm the oven to 350 degrees.
2. Stir the baking soda, flour, and salt in a small bowl. Set aside.
3. Use a blender, cream, butter, and sugar. Put the vanilla and egg, and mix until just combined. Gently blend the dry combination into the creamed combination. Whisk in the chocolate chips, coconut flakes, and sliced almonds.
4. Using a 1 ½ tbsp cookie scoop, place rounded spoonful's onto parchment-covered baking sheets. Bake for approximately nine to twelve minutes. Let to cool for ten minutes prior to moving to the cookie cooling racks.

47. SMALL BATCH BUTTER COOKIES

Prep Time: 10 Mins

Cook Time: 10 Mins

Cool Time: 5 Mins

Total Time: 25 Mins

Servings: 6

Ingredients

- 4 tbsp salted softened butter
- 3 tbsp granulated sugar
- ½ cup of all-purpose flour
- 1 large egg yolk
- ½ tsp vanilla extract
- walnuts optional topping (can also use pecans, sanding sugar, melted chocolate, and sprinkles)

Instructions

1. Set the oven's temperature to 350 °F (177°C). Use parchment paper to line a small baking tray.
2. In a medium-sized mixing bowl, blend the butter and the sugar together with a hand blender until creamy, approximately one to two minutes.
3. Put the egg yolk and vanilla and combine thoroughly.
4. Put in the flour and mix on low until well mixed.
5. Scoop the cookie dough with a medium-sized cookie scoop or a big tbsp and set it on the baking sheet, spacing it two inches apart.
6. Make spherical balls of cookie dough.
7. Slowly press down on each dough ball with the bottom of a drinking glass.
8. If you're using pecans or walnuts, press one into the middle of each cookie carefully. Distribute with sanding sugar, if using, and bake for about eight to ten minutes or until the edges start to brown slightly.
9. Take from the oven and let the cookies rest for five minutes on the baking sheet.
10. To continue chilling, move the cookies to a cooling rack.

48. SMALL BATCH TRIPLE CHOCOLATE COOKIES

Prep Time: 10 Mins

Cook Time: 8 Mins

Total Time: 18 Mins

Servings: 6

Ingredients

- 4 tbsp cubed cold salted butter
- ¼ cup of packed brown sugar
- 3 tbsp granulated sugar
- 1 large egg yolk
- ½ tsp vanilla extract
- ½ cup of scooped and leveled all-purpose flour
- 2 tbsp unsweetened cocoa powder
- ¼ tsp baking powder
- ¼ tsp baking soda
- ¼ tsp salt
- ½ cup of chocolate chips, white chocolate, a mix of milk chocolate, and semisweet chocolate

Instructions

1. Warm the oven to 400°F. Use parchment paper to line a cooking sheet.
2. In a stand blender fitted with the paddle attachment or using a handheld blender, beat the butter, brown sugar, and granulated sugar for two to three minutes until creamy and light. Put the egg yolk and vanilla, and beat again, stopping to scrape the bowl's bottom and sides.
3. Combine flour, baking soda, cocoa powder, baking powder, and salt. Mix again just until combined. Whisk in milk chocolate, semisweet, and white chocolate chips.
4. Split the dough evenly into four large or six regular-sized cookies, spacing them a couple of inches apart on the cooking sheet so they have room to spread. Put it in the oven for eight to nine minutes or until the edges are set and the top is no longer shiny. For decorating, press a few more chips onto the top of each biscuit while it is still hot from the oven.
5. Cool for five to ten minutes on the baking sheet prior to moving to a wire rack to cool fully. Enjoy!

49. VEGAN CHOCOLATE CHIP COOKIES

Total Time: 22 Mins

Servings: 6

Ingredients

- ¾ cup of all-purpose flour
- ½ tsp baking powder
- ⅛ tsp baking soda
- ½ tsp kosher salt
- ½ cup of sifted coconut sugar
- 2 ½ tbsp neutral oil
- 2 tbsp nut or plant-based milk
- 1 cup of dark chocolate chips

Instructions

1. Warm the oven to 350°F and prepare a baking sheet with parchment paper.
2. In a big bowl, put baking powder, baking soda, flour, and salt and whisk to mix.
3. Put in the oil, nut milk, and coconut sugar. Allow the coconut oil to cool a little if using melted oil prior to adding it. Use a spatula to fold the ingredients together until there are no crumbs.
4. Fold in the chocolate chips. The combination, unlike traditional cookie dough, will be thick, making it easier to mix with your hands. Shape the dough into six balls and put them on a baking tray.
5. Bake until golden, twelve to fourteen minutes. Let cool for five minutes until they harden a bit. Enjoy!

50. OATMEAL COOKIES WITH ICING

Prep Time: 10 Mins

Cook Time: 12 Mins

Total Time: 50 Mins

Servings: 6

Ingredients

Small-Batch Oatmeal Cookies

- ½ cup of uncooked oats (quick-cook or old-fashioned)
- ½ cup of all-purpose flour
- ¾ tsp baking powder
- ¼ tsp baking soda
- ⅛ tsp salt
- 1 tsp cinnamon
- ⅛ tsp nutmeg
- 4 tbsp unsalted butter (melted & slightly cooled)
- ¼ cup of granulated sugar
- 2 tbsp brown sugar
- 1 large egg yolk
- ½ tsp vanilla extract

Vanilla Icing (Optional)

- ⅓ cup of powdered sugar
- ¼ tsp vanilla extract
- 1-2 tsp milk

Instructions

Small-Batch Oatmeal Cookies

1. Warm the oven to 350°F and prepare one cooking sheet with parchment paper or a silicone baking mat.
2. In a food processor, pulse oatmeal about five to six times until it's slightly chopped but not totally ground. Set aside.
3. In a small bowl, stir baking powder, baking soda, salt, flour, cinnamon, nutmeg, and processed oatmeal.

4. In a medium bowl, stir together melted, granulated sugar, slightly cooled butter, and brown sugar until smooth.
5. Stir in egg yolk and vanilla until completely mixed. Stir in the flour and oatmeal combination with a spoon until well combined.
6. Drop six rounded spoonful's (approximately 1.5 ounces each) onto the prepared baking sheet as widely apart as possible (these cookies spread) and bake until just set, 12 minutes for softer cookies, fourteen to sixteen minutes for crispy cookies. Cool on the baking sheet until comfortable to handle. Completely cool if icing.

Icing

7. In a small bowl, stir vanilla extract, powdered sugar, and one tsp of milk. Just add enough milk, up to 1 tsp more, to get a drizzling consistency. Spoon over the cooled cookies. Allow the frosting to set for at least fifteen minutes, then enjoy!

51. EASIEST SMALL BATCH CHOCOLATE CHIP COOKIES WITH BROWN BUTTER AND SEA SALT

Prep Time: 15 Mins

Cook Time: 12 Mins

Total Time: 27 Mins

Servings: 8

Ingredients

- 6 tbsp browned salted butter
- ⅔ cup of packed light brown sugar
- 1 large egg
- 1 tsp pure vanilla extract
- 1 cup of all-purpose flour (add an additional 2 tbsp flour for slightly thicker cookies)
- 1 tsp cornstarch
- ½ tsp baking soda
- 4 Ounces chopped semi-sweet or bittersweet chocolate (baking bar, 60%-70% cacao)
- flaky sea salt for sprinkling (optional)

Instructions

1. Let to cool a little.
2. Whisk the cooled brown butter and brown sugar in a big bowl until thoroughly combined.
3. When the combination has thickened and lightened in color, add the egg and beat thoroughly. Mix in the vanilla extract.
4. In a separate bowl, stir flour, cornstarch, and baking soda.
5. Incorporate the dry ingredients completely into the wet ones by folding them in.
6. Fold in the chopped chocolate, including small pieces and shards.
7. Wrap the dough with plastic wrap and chill in the refrigerator for at least an hour or up to overnight.
8. To make 2½ tbsp-sized balls, use a #30 cookie scoop or spoon and place on a large baking sheet coated with parchment paper or silicone baking liner.
9. Warm the oven to 375° F. While the oven is preheating, set the baking sheet with the dough balls in the freezer for ten minutes.
10. Put the cookie sheet in the oven, and then lower the temperature right away to 350°F.
11. Bake the cookies at 350°F for twelve minutes or until the edges are golden brown. Take after ten minutes for a gooier and more undercooked interior.
12. If desired, distribute the cookies with flaky sea salt. Allow cookies to cool for about fifteen minutes on the cookie sheet, then gently move them to a wire rack to cool completely.

52. SMALL BATCH NO BAKE COOKIES

Prep Time: 5 Mins

Cook Time: 1 Min

Inactive Time: 25 Mins

Total Time: 31 Mins

Serving: 6

Ingredients

- ⅛ cup of butter
- ½ cup of sugar
- ⅛ cup of milk
- 1 tbsp cocoa powder
- ⅛ cup of peanut butter
- 1 cup of quick-cooking oats
- ½ tsp vanilla

Instructions

1. In a saucepan on a medium-high flame, combine the butter, sugar, milk, and cocoa powder. Put the combination to a rolling boil, then let it sit for one minute.
2. After one minute, take from the flame and add the peanut butter, oats, and vanilla.
3. Put the combination on wax or parchment paper using a cookie scoop and let it cool until it sets. You may speed up this process by letting the cookies chill in the refrigerator.

53. BEST OATMEAL CHOCOLATE CHIP COOKIES

Prep Time: 10 Mins

Cook Time: 10 Mins

Total Time: 20 Mins

Serving: 6

Ingredients

- 6 tbsp unsalted softened butter
- ¼ cup of dark brown sugar
- 3 tbsp granulated sugar
- 1 large egg yolk only
- ¾ tsp vanilla extract
- ½ cup of all-purpose flour
- ¼ cup of rolled oats
- ⅛ tsp fine salt
- ¼ tsp baking soda
- ¼ tsp baking powder
- ⅓ cup of chocolate chips

Instructions

1. Warm the oven to 375 degrees. Line a baking sheet with a light-colored silicone mat.
2. In a medium bowl, use an electric blender to blend the butter on medium speed until fluffy, approximately twenty seconds.
3. Add the sugar and beat for about thirty seconds. The combination will turn a pale color and be fluffy.
4. Next, put the egg yolk and vanilla and blend until just blended.
5. In a separate bowl, whisk flour, oats, salt, baking soda, and powder.
6. Distribute the flour on top of the butter combination, and beat just until mixed.
7. Whisk in the chocolate chips.
8. Scoop the dough into six big dough balls and arrange them evenly on the cooking sheet.
9. Bake for ten to eleven minutes, removing the cookies once the edges begin to turn golden brown.
10. Allow the cookies to rest on the cooking sheet for one minute prior to moving them to a wire rack to cool.

54. CHOCOLATE CHIP WALNUT COOKIES

Prep Time: 5 Mins

Cook Time: 12 Mins

Chilling Time: 30 Mins

Total Time: 47 Mins

Serving: 4

Ingredients

- 1¼ cups of all-purpose flour
- ½ tsp kosher salt
- ¼ tsp baking soda
- ⅓ cup of unsalted melted butter
- ¼ cup of brown sugar
- ¼ cup of granulated sugar
- 1 large egg
- 1 tbsp vanilla extract
- ¾ cup of chocolate chips with a few saved for post-bake
- ½ cup of chopped walnuts
- flakey sea salt post-bake

Instructions

1. In a medium bowl, whisk the all-purpose flour, salt, and baking soda.
2. In a large bowl, mix together the butter, sugars, egg, and vanilla. Add the dried ingredients and whisk until everything is combined. Finally, whisk in the chocolate chips and walnuts.
3. Split the dough into four even balls (about 145g each) and roll into spheres - put on a lined platter or baking tray. Put your dough in the refrigerator overnight, or at least for thirty minutes, to improve the texture, flavor, and spread of the cookie once it's time to bake.
4. Use parchment paper to prepare your baking sheets. Set the cookies about three to four inches apart on your baking sheets.
5. Warm the oven to 350 degrees and bake the cookies, one sheet at a time, for about thirteen to fifteen minutes, until the edges are hard and the interiors are soft. These are large cookies, so they will take some time to bake through!
6. Distribute cookies with flakey sea salt, chill them on a wire rack, and enjoy!

55. PEPPERMINT BARK COOKIES

Prep Time: 5 Mins

Cook Time: 15 Mins

Decorating Time: 5 Mins

Total Time: 25 Mins

Serving: 8

Ingredients

- 1 tbsp coconut oil
- 2 tbsp nut or seed butter
- 3 tbsp maple syrup
- ½ tsp vanilla extract
- ½ cup of flour gf all-purpose if desired
- 2 tbsp cocoa powder
- ⅛ tsp baking soda
- ⅛ tsp salt

Chocolate Coating

- ¼ cup of white chocolate chips or candy melts dairy-free if desired
- 1 tsp coconut oil
- peppermint extract to taste

Instructions

1. Warm the oven to 350°F and prepare a cookie sheet with parchment paper.
2. In a large bowl, warm the coconut oil. Add the nut butter (assuming it is at room temperature) and mix until smooth.
3. Put the maple syrup and vanilla extract and mix well. If your coconut oil has hardened, slowly microwave it to make it liquid again.
4. If the cocoa powder is clumpy, sift it in and mix it in until it's smooth.
5. Make a well in the center, then add the flour, baking soda, and salt. Mix them into the flour roughly. Mix flour with the wet stuff and form your chocolate cookie dough.
6. Make walnut-sized balls with your palms and flatten them gently on a baking sheet.
7. Bake for eight minutes, then take them out of the oven, let them cool fully, and stick them in the freezer or fridge to get them cold.

8. Warm your chocolate and coconut oil together (I microwave it in 30-second increments). The idea is to create a thin sauce. If the sauce still seems too thick, add additional coconut oil. Combine in your peppermint extract.
9. Dip the top of each cooled cookie and coat it with approximately a tsp of chocolate (there will be some left over to use later). (Optional: distribute with a crushed candy cane).
10. Allow the covered cookies to cool again in the fridge. Enjoy!!

56. CARAMEL PECAN THUMBPRINT COOKIES

Prep Time: 20 Mins

Cook Time: 14 Mins

Total Time: 34 Mins

Serving: 12

Ingredients

For the Cookies

- 1 cup of all-purpose flour
- ¼ tsp baking soda
- ¼ tsp salt
- ½ cup of unsalted softened butter
- ⅓ cup of firmly packed light brown sugar
- 1 large separated egg
- ½ tsp vanilla extract
- ¾ cup of finely chopped pecans

For the Caramel Filling

- 2 ounces soft caramels
- 1 ½ tbsp heavy cream

Instructions

To Make the Cookies

1. Warm the oven to 350 degrees Fahrenheit. Use parchment paper to line a cooking sheet.
2. Stir the baking soda, flour, and salt. Set aside.

3. Put the electric blender on medium speed and beat the brown sugar and butter together until they are light and fluffy. Add the egg yolk and combine thoroughly. Mix in the vanilla.
4. Add the flour combination, and mix just until mixed.
5. Roll out the dough into balls, one tbsp at a time.
6. Put the egg white in one tiny, shallow bowl and the pecans in another shallow one.
7. Coat each ball of dough with egg white and then roll in pecans.
8. Put the cookies on the ready pan, leaving about two inches between the cookies. In the center of each ball of dough, make an indentation with the end of a wooden spoon.
9. Bake for twelve to fourteen minutes or until well browned.
10. Cool the cookies in the pan on a wire rack for ten minutes. (If necessary, delicately reshape the indentation in the cookies immediately after they come out of the oven.) Then, move the cookies to a wire rack to thoroughly cool.

To Make the Caramel Filling

11. In a microwave-safe bowl, put the caramels and the cream.
12. Warm at half power for thirty seconds at a time until the caramels are melted. (Alternatively, warm on medium-low on the stove until melted.) Whisk until smooth.
13. Fill the indentations in the cooled cookies with caramel. Let for the filling to set prior to serving.

57. CHOCOLATE CRINKLE COOKIES

Prep Time: 10 Mins

Cook Time: 10 Mins

Chill Time: 1 Hr

Total Time: 1 Hr 20 Mins

Serving: 8

Ingredients

- ¼ cup of granulated sugar
- 3 tbsp dark brown sugar
- 2 tbsp canola oil
- 1 large egg room temperature
- ½ tsp vanilla extract
- ½ cup of all-purpose flour
- ¼ cup of unsweetened cocoa powder (Dutch process)
- ½ tsp baking powder
- ¼ tsp salt
- ¼ cup of semi-sweet chocolate chips
- 2 tbsp powdered sugar for rolling the cookies

Instructions

1. In a medium mixing bowl, mix granulated sugar, brown sugar, and canola oil. Mix until well mixed. Put the egg and vanilla and mix until mixed and smooth.
2. Over the wet ingredients, sift the flour, cocoa powder, baking powder, and salt. Whisk just until no dry streaks remain. Note: I recommend sifting the dried ingredients over the wet components to ensure there are no lumps, especially with the cocoa powder.
3. Put the chocolate chips and stir just until combined. It will be a sticky dough. To chill for at least an hour, cover the bowl and put it in the fridge.
4. Warm the oven to 350°F and put the oven rack in the center position. Use parchment paper to line a cooking sheet.
5. In a shallow dish, combine the powdered sugar.

6. Scoop even amounts of cold cookie dough and shape it into a ball with your hands (the dough may still be sticky). Roll each cookie dough ball generously in powdered sugar twice. Put the cookies on the prepared cooking sheet, at least two inches apart. Note that the number of cookies you get will be determined by the size of the cookie scoop you use.
7. Bake the cookies for approximately ten to twelve minutes - or until the edges are firm and the center still looks 'un-done.' Cool the cookies for five minutes on the baking sheet, then transfer to a wire cooling rack. Then, move the cookies to a wire rack to thoroughly cool. Enjoy!

58. SMALL BATCH RICOTTA COOKIES

Prep Time: 10 Mins

Cook Time: 12 Mins

Total Time: 22 Mins

Serving: 8

Ingredients

- 2 tbsp softened butter
- 4 tbsp granulated sugar
- 1 large egg yolk
- 2 tbsp ricotta cheese
- ⅛ tsp vanilla extract
- ½ cup of all-purpose flour
- ¼ tsp baking powder

For the Glaze

- 3 tbsp powdered sugar
- 1 tsp milk
- ⅛ tsp vanilla extract
- optional: sprinkles

Instructions

1. Set oven temperature to 350°F, or 177°C.
2. In a medium-sized bowl, mix sugar and softened butter. Mix with an electric hand blender at medium speed for approximately one minute or until thoroughly combined.
3. Add the egg yolk, ricotta, and ⅛ tsp of the vanilla and keep beating until well mixed.
4. Put the flour and baking powder to the bowl and combine on low speed until dough begins to form.
5. Use a 2-tbsp cookie scoop to transfer the dough to a baking sheet coated with silpat or parchment paper. Bake for twelve to fifteen minutes or until the cookies are golden on the bottom.
6. Cool the cookies on the cooking sheet for approximately three to four minutes, then remove to a cooling rack to cool fully.
7. To make the glaze
8. In a small bowl, stir milk, powdered sugar, and ⅛ tsp of vanilla. Spoon the glaze over each cookie.
9. Top with distributes if desired, or enjoy as is.

59. SMALL BATCH OF SUGAR COOKIES

Prep Time: 10 Mins

Cook Time: 10 Mins

Total Time: 20 Mins

Serving: 6

Ingredients

- 3 tbsp butter
- 4 tbsp granulated sugar
- 1 egg yolk
- ½ tbsp corn syrup
- ½ tsp vanilla extract
- ⅔ cup + 2 tbsp all-purpose flour
- ⅛ tsp baking soda
- ⅛ tsp salt

Instructions

1. Warm the oven to 350°F. Add parchment paper or a silicone cooking mat to the baking sheet to line it. Set aside.
2. In the bowl of a stand blender or with an electric hand blender, cream together the butter and sugar until well mixed.
3. Scrape the sides of the bowl, and next add the egg yolk, corn syrup, and vanilla. Mix until well mixed.
4. Combine the baking soda, flour, and salt, and mix until a dough form.
5. Split the dough into six equal-sized portions and roll into balls.
6. Bake at 350° F for seven to nine minutes or until the middle of the cookies no longer look wet and glossy.
7. Let the cookies to cool completely on the pan.
8. Keep it in an airtight jar for up to three days.

60. SMALL-BATCH PEANUT BUTTER COOKIES

Prep Time: 10 Mins

Cook Time: 10 Mins

Total Time: 20 Mins

Serving: 6

Ingredients

- ½ cup of all-purpose flour
- ¼ tsp baking soda
- ¼ tsp salt
- ⅓ cup of peanut butter (not natural peanut butter)
- 3 tbsp unsalted softened butter
- 3 tbsp brown sugar
- 2 tbsp granulated sugar
- 1 large egg yolk
- ½ tsp vanilla extract

Instructions

1. Warm the oven to 350°F and prepare a cooking sheet with parchment paper.
2. In a small bowl, stir baking soda, flour, and salt.
3. In a medium bowl, mix peanut butter, softened butter, egg yolk, brown sugar, granulated sugar, and vanilla. Stir together until smooth.
4. Stir in the flour combination until it is just combined. Take round spoonfuls of the dough and roll them into six balls. Put the dough on the ready cookie sheet and use a fork to tightly press a crosshatch pattern on the tops of the cookies.
5. For eight to eleven minutes, or until the sides look set but the cookies are still pale, bake them. For crispier cookies, bake them for ten to twelve minutes or until they start to turn darker. Cool on the cooking sheet for at least ten minutes prior to moving (cookies will be quite tender until they cool).
6. Enjoy!

(BARS RECIPES)

61. SMALL BATCH BROOKIE BARS RECIPE

Prep Time: 10 Mins

Cook Time: 24 Mins

Total Time: 20 Mins

Serving: 6

Ingredients

For the Chocolate Chip Cookie Dough

- ½ cup plus 1 tbsp all-purpose flour
- ¼ tsp baking soda
- ¼ tsp kosher salt
- 3 tbsp unsalted butter
- ⅓ cup of tightly packed light brown sugar
- 1 large egg yolk
- ¼ tsp pure vanilla extract
- ½ cup of bittersweet

For the Brownie Batter

- ¾ cup of granulated sugar
- ⅓ cup of all-purpose flour
- ⅓ cup of Dutch-processed or natural unsweetened cocoa powder, sifted if necessary
- ¼ cup of sifted confectioners' sugar, if necessary
- ½ tsp kosher salt
- 4 tbsp unsalted butter
- 1 large egg
- ¼ tsp pure vanilla extract
- 1 tbsp boiling water
- flaky salt for garnish

Instructions

For the Small Batch Brookie Bars

1. **Prep your oven and pans:** Position a rack in the middle of the oven and warm the oven to 350°F. Then, lightly spray cooking spray on a 9-by-5-inch loaf pan and layer it with parchment paper, leaving two inches of extra on each long side. Sprinkle the parchment, too.
2. **Make the chocolate chip cookie dough:** Whisk the baking soda, flour, and salt in a medium bowl.
3. In a medium, heatproof bowl, warm the butter at 15- to 20-second intervals, stirring as required with a heatproof rubber spatula. Put the brown sugar over the melted butter and combine with a heatproof rubber spatula until just combined. Once melted, add the egg yolk and vanilla and mix until it is just combined. Slowly mix in the dried ingredients and mix until it's just combined. Add the chocolate and mix until it's spread out evenly.
4. **Start assembling the brookie bars:** Use a 1-tbsp cookie dough scoop, divide half of the cookie dough into balls, and drop them randomly into the prepared loaf pan as you go. Press down gently on each cookie dough ball. Keep half of the cookie dough aside for the topping of the brookie bars.
5. **Make the brownie batter:** In a medium bowl, stir confectioners' sugar, granulated sugar, flour, cocoa powder, and salt.
6. Warm the butter in a medium heatproof bowl at 15- to 20-second intervals, stirring as required with a heatproof rubber spatula. Once melted, add the egg and vanilla and combine until it's just mixed. Slowly mix in the dried ingredients and mix until it's just combined. Mix in the water just until it's mixed.
7. **Finish assembling the brookie bars:** Put the batter into the prepared pan containing the cookie dough and smooth the surface with an offset spatula, covering the cookie dough pieces. Distribute generous pinches of the remaining chocolate chip cookie dough over the batter. Gently push down on the pieces to combine them with the brownie batter.
8. **Bake the brookie bars:** Bake for fifty to fifty-five minutes, or until a skewer inserted into the middle of the brownies comes up with a few crumbs attached. Check the bars at about thirty minutes into the Bake Time; if the cookie dough is browning too soon, cover the pan with a loose layer of aluminum foil. Let chill fully on a wire rack before slicing.

9. **Serve and store:** Lift out the brookie bars, use the overhanging paper as handles, and place them on a cutting board. Run your butter knife or offset spatula along the sides of the pan. Cut into eight petite squares or two large bakery-style bars according to the baker's instructions. Serve with flaky salt as a garnish. The brookie bars can be kept in an airtight container or zip-top bag at room temp for up to three days.

62. HOMEMADE LEMON BARS (EASY LEMON BAR RECIPE)

Prep Time: 20 Mins

Cook Time: 50 Mins

Total Time: 1 Hr 10 Mins

Serving: 6

Ingredients

For the Shortbread Crust

- 12 tbsp cold unsalted butter
- ½ cup of powdered sugar
- 1½ cups of flour
- pinch of salt

For the Lemon Filling

- 1 cup of granulated sugar
- 2 tsp packed lemon zest
- 6 tbsp fresh lemon juice
- 2 large eggs
- 2 large egg yolks
- ½ tsp baking powder
- 2 tbsp flour
- powdered sugar for sprinkling

Instructions

1. Warm the oven to 350°. A glass bread loaf pan that is 9" x 5" x 3" works best for these bars. If all you have is a metal loaf pan, line it completely with parchment paper. You don't want the acidic lemon curd touching the sides of the metal pan.

2. **First, make the shortbread crust:** Put all crust ingredients in a medium bowl. To mix the butter with the sugar, flour, and salt, you can use your fingers or a pastry cutter. You should have a coarse meal. Press this combination firmly into the bottom of the loaf pan. Bake for twenty-five minutes or until the sides are gently browned and the top is not damp to the touch.
3. When you remove the pan from the oven, you can begin preparing your filling. (Do not create the filling ahead of time and set it aside—eggs and lemon juice do not mix well). In a small bowl, mix the whole egg, granulated sugar, lemon juice, lemon zest, and egg yolk with a hand-held electric blender. Mix this combination very well until it becomes frothy--about one minute.
4. Put the baking powder and flour and mix until no lumps remain. Put the combination over the crust that has been cooling. Return the pan to the oven for an additional 20-23 minutes or until the filling is firm.
5. Take the bars immediately from the loaf pan and allow them to cool prior to dusting them with powdered sugar and slicing them into bars.

63. SMALL BATCH MAGIC COOKIE BARS RECIPE

Prep Time: 5 Mins

Cook Time: 15 Mins

Bake Time: 22 Mins

Total Time: 20 Mins

Serving: 1

Ingredients

For the Magic Cookie Bars

- ⅓ cup of pecans (roughly chopped into ¼- to ½-inch pieces)
- ⅔ cup of salted caramel biscotti cookie crumbs
- 3 tbsp unsalted melted butter
- ⅔ cup of sweetened condensed milk
- ½ cup of bittersweet or extra-dark chocolate chips
- ⅓ cup of sweetened flaked coconut
- flaky sea salt

Instructions

For the Small Batch Magic Cookie Bars

1. **Prep your oven and pan:** Set up a rack in the middle of the oven and heat it up to 350°F. Sprinkle a 9-by-5-inch loaf pan generously with cooking spray and accordance it with parchment paper, leaving a two-inch overhang on two long sides of the pan. Sprinkle the parchment, too.
2. **Toast the nuts:** Use parchment paper to line a quarter sheet pan. Sprinkle the pecans out in a single layer on the pan. Bake until fragrant and toasted brown, about five to ten minutes. To ensure even toasting, toss the nuts every two to three minutes with a heatproof rubber spatula. Scrape the nuts onto a platter when they are toasted to prevent them from cooking any further.
3. **Make the biscotti crust:** In a medium bowl, mix the Nonni's Salted Caramel Biscotti cookie crumbs and melted butter. Toss the combination with a rubber spatula until it is the consistency of wet sand. Put the combination into the prepared pan and push it evenly across the bottom, all the way to the edges. (You may use the bottom of a coffee mug or heavy glass to pound the crumbs into place—you want to apply some pressure here so the crust keeps its shape.)
4. **Assemble the bars:** Put the sweetened condensed milk over the crust and sprinkle it evenly with an offset spatula, smoothing the top. Distribute half of the chocolate chips and coconut over the milk. Distribute all of the nuts over the chocolate and coconut, followed by the remaining chocolate and coconut halves. To bind the ingredients to the sweetened condensed milk, gently press on top of them with your palms.
5. **Bake the bars:** Bake for twenty-two to twenty-four minutes, or until the sides of the bar are firm and bubbling, but the center still wobbles a little. Put the bars on a wire rack and sprinkle with flaky sea salt. Cool for another fifteen minutes, then use a butter knife or offset spatula to run around the pan's edges. Keep chilling the bars fully.
6. **Serve and store:** When the bars have cooled, use the overhanging parchment as handles to pull them out of the pan and onto a cutting board. To slice and serve, use a heated knife. The magic cookie bars can be kept in an airtight jar on the counter for up to three days.

64. SMALL BATCH PEANUT BUTTER BARS

Prep Time: 10 Mins

Chill Time: 2 Hrs

Total Time: 2 Hrs 10 Mins

Serving: 4

Ingredients

- ¼ cup of butter (melted and slightly cooled)
- ¼ cup of creamy peanut butter
- 6 tbsp sifted powdered sugar
- ½ cup of graham cracker crumbs

For the topping

- ⅓ cup of semi-sweet chocolate chips
- 1 tbsp creamy peanut butter

Instructions

1. Put parchment paper into a 5 × 5-inch baking dish.
2. To a medium-sized bowl, add the melted butter.
3. Add the peanut butter to the bowl and use an electric hand blender on low speed to combine until smooth.
4. Sift the powdered sugar and place it in the bowl.
5. Mix on low speed until well combined. To mix all the powdered sugar in, make sure to scrape the sides of the bowl.
6. Mix the Graham cracker crumbs in with a rubber spatula until everything is well mixed.
7. Put into the lined baking dish and then distribute the batter evenly in the pan.
8. Make the topping. In a microwave-safe bowl, put the chocolate chips and peanut butter. Microwave on high for twenty to twenty-five seconds, whisking in between each burst, until the chocolate is melted and the combination is smooth.
9. Sprinkle the chocolate and peanut butter topping to the boundaries of the peanut butter base in an even manner.
10. Chill in the fridge until firm, for at least two hours. Get the parchment paper out of the dish.
11. Cut into squares and enjoy!

65. MINI-BATCH TWIX BARS

Prep Time: 5 Mins

Cook Time: 15 Mins

Freezing Time: 1 Hr

Total Time: 1 Hr 20 Mins

Serving: 6

Ingredients

Cookie layer

- 1 tbsp coconut oil
- 1 tbsp maple syrup
- ½ cup of almond flour
- drop of vanilla
- pinch of salt

Caramel layer

- 1 tbsp nut or seed butter
- 1 tbsp maple syrup
- 1 tsp coconut oil
- drop of vanilla
- pinch of salt

Chocolate coating

- ¼ cup of chocolate chips
- 1 tsp coconut oil

Instructions

1. Warm the oven to 350° Fahrenheit and line a small baking tray with paper. Mine is three inches by 5.75 inches.
2. In a bowl, mix coconut oil and microwave until melted. Combine the maple, vanilla, and salt with a stir. To make a dough, add almond flour.
3. Push the cookie dough evenly onto the pan and bake for twenty-five minutes or until the edges are slightly browned. Completely cool.
4. In a small bowl, add caramel ingredients and melt in the microwave; whisk to mix until smooth. Put over the cookie crust and freeze to set fully for at least one hour.

5. When the bars are set, cut them into six and put them back in the freezer.
6. Microwave the chocolate-coating ingredients for thirty seconds at a time, stirring until the chocolate is completely melted. Dip each frozen bar in chocolate, then put it back on the paper and freeze/refrigerate to set the chocolate.
7. Enjoy the bars! Keep them in the freezer or refrigerator. I eat them directly from the freezer, like a frozen treat.

66. CHOCOLATE CHUNK COOKIE BARS

Prep Time: 10 Mins

Cook Time: 20 Mins

Total Time: 30 Mins

Serving: 8

Ingredients

- 90 g all-purpose flour
- ¼ tsp baking powder
- ¼ tsp baking soda
- ¼ tsp fine sea salt
- 60 g unsalted butter
- 55 g dark brown sugar
- 45 g granulated sugar
- 1 large egg yolk
- ½ tsp vanilla extract
- 115 g chopped dark chocolate (70% cacao)
- flaky sea salt (optional)

Instructions

1. Set oven temperature to 350°F, or 180°C. To grease a 9x5-inch loaf pan, use butter or nonstick cooking spray. Next, put parchment paper around the pan, leaving extra on all sides. Set aside the parchment paper after greasing it with butter or nonstick frying spray.
2. In a small bowl, stir together the flour, baking powder, baking soda, and salt. Set aside.

3. In a medium bowl, combine the butter, dark brown sugar, and granulated sugar and blend with an electric hand blender until thoroughly combined and fluffy, about three minutes.
4. Mix in egg yolk and vanilla until thoroughly combined. Add the dried ingredients and mix until it's just combined. Fold in the chopped chocolate to the dough.
5. Press the dough slowly into an even layer in the prepared pan. Bake for fifteen to eighteen minutes or until the top is softly golden brown and firm to the touch. (It is best to slightly under bake rather than overbake!) Just as the pan is taking the pan out of the oven, distribute flaky sea salt on top if desired. Let the cookie bars to cool completely in the pan prior to removing and slicing.
6. Cover and keep leftover bars in an airtight jar at room temperature for two to three days.

67. PEANUT BUTTER BARS RECIPE

Prep Time: 15 Mins

Cook Time: 15 Mins

Total Time: 30 Mins

Servings: 6

Ingredients

- 3 tbsp brown sugar
- 3 tbsp sugar
- 3 tbsp salted butter
- ½ cup of divided peanut butter plus 2 tbsp
- 1 tbsp egg beaten
- ¼ tsp vanilla
- ¼ tsp baking soda
- pinch of salt
- ¼ cup of all-purpose flour plus 2 tbsp
- ¼ cup of old-fashioned oats

Chocolate Frosting

- 2 tbsp softened butter
- 1 tbsp milk
- ½ tsp vanilla

- 1 tbsp cocoa
- ¾ cup of powdered sugar

Instructions

1. Warm the oven to 350 degrees F.
2. Lightly grease nine by seven baking pan
3. Cream the butter and sugars together in a bowl.
4. Combine beaten egg, ¼ cup of peanut butter, and vanilla.
5. Combine oats, flour, baking soda, and a bit of salt.
6. Sprinkle evenly in the pan and bake for fifteen minutes.
7. Take from the oven and top with tsp of the remaining peanut butter. Let to soften and melt completely prior to spreading.
8. Gently spread softened peanut butter on top of the warm bars. Let the bars to cool.
9. Combine the frosting ingredients and put them on top of the cooled bars.

68. CHOCOLATE CHIP COOKIE BARS

Prep Time: 15 Mins

Cook Time: 23 Mins

Total Time: 38 Mins

Servings: 6-8

Ingredients

- ¾ cup of all-purpose flour
- ¼ tsp baking soda
- ¼ tsp baking powder
- ¼ tsp salt
- ¼ cup of unsalted softened butter
- ¼ cup of packed brown sugar
- 2 tbsp granulated sugar
- 1 egg yolk room temperature
- ½ tsp vanilla extract
- ½ cup of semisweet chocolate chips

Instructions

1. Warm the oven to 350 °F. Use parchment paper to line a 9-by-5-inch loaf pan.
2. In a medium bowl, stir the baking powder, flour, baking soda, and salt.
3. Beat the brown sugar, butter, and sugar together in a big mixing bowl on medium speed for approximately two minutes or until smooth and creamy.
4. Mix in the yolk and vanilla until smooth.
5. Mix in the flour combination gradually on low speed for one minute or until the dough comes together. The combination will appear dry and crumbly, but it will come together and pat into the pan. Don't overbeat. Whisk in the chocolate chips.
6. Pat the dough into the pan evenly. Bake for eighteen to twenty-three minutes or until puffed and golden brown. Let it cool for fifteen minutes prior to removing it from the pan. Completely cool prior to cutting.

69. SMALL BATCH LEMON BARS

Total Time: 1 Hr 10 Mins

Servings: 16

Ingredients

Crust Ingredients

- ½ cup of salted softened butter
- ½ cup of powdered sugar
- 1 cup of all-purpose flour

Lemon Filling Ingredients

- 3 eggs
- 1½ cups of sugar
- 2 fresh lemons zest
- ½ cup of fresh lemon juice
- ½ cup of all-purpose flour
- ¼ tsp vanilla (optional)
- additional powdered sugar for dusting

Instructions

1. Warm the oven to 350°F. Sprinkle or line a 9-by-9-inch square pan with cooking spray or parchment paper, as recommended. In a medium mixing bowl, mix flour, butter, and powdered sugar with a pastry blender until well combined. Mix until coarse crumbs form, but the dough is not cohesive.
2. Evenly press the base into the pan. Bake the crust for approximately fifteen minutes. Let it cool a little.
3. While the crust is baking, in a medium mixing bowl, stir the eggs and sugar until combined. Keep whisking in the lemon juice, lemon zest, flour, and vanilla until completely smooth.
4. Put the filling over the crust when it has cooled for five minutes (it will still be hot), then return to the oven. Bake until the filling is set, approximately twenty-three to twenty-five minutes.
5. Let cool thoroughly prior to cutting into bars. Keep it in the refrigerator.
6. Sprinkle with powdered sugar right before serving. If preferred, serve with whipped cream and fresh raspberries.

70. MAGIC COOKIE BARS, SMALL BATCH

Total Time: 50 Mins

Servings: 8

Ingredients

- 60 g melted butter
- 90 g digestive biscuit crumbs or graham cracker crumbs
- 65 g chopped toasted pecans
- 90 g semi-sweet chocolate chips
- 90 g white chocolate chips
- 90 g butterscotch or peanut butter chips
- 60 g sweetened shredded coconut
- 200 g sweetened condensed milk

Instructions

1. Set oven temperature to 180 degrees C (350°F) or gas mark 4. Sprinkle canola cooking spray on aluminum foil and line a 7-by-11-inch baking dish with it. Set aside.

2. Combine the crumbs and melted butter. Press them into an equal layer at the bottom of the dish.
3. Distribute with the toasted pecans and then the various chips, distributing them out evenly.
4. Evenly distribute the sweetened condensed milk over everything.
5. Finally, distribute the coconut over the top.
6. Bake in the heated oven for fifteen to twenty minutes or until the top is lightly golden brown.
7. Let cool thoroughly prior to cutting into bars. (I placed mine in the refrigerator for about an hour before I sliced them, lifted them out by the tinfoil, and then cut them.)

71. SUGAR COOKIE BARS WITH CREAM CHEESE

Prep Time: 20 Mins

Cook Time: 20 Mins

Total Time: 40 Mins

Servings: 9

Ingredients

- ½ cup of unsalted softened butter
- ¾ cup of granulated sugar
- 1 large egg
- 1 ½ tsp vanilla extract
- 1¾ cups of all-purpose flour
- ½ tsp baking powder
- ¼ tsp salt

For the Frosting

- 4 tbsp unsalted softened butter
- 3 ounces whipped cream cheese
- ¾ tsp vanilla extract
- 2 cups of powdered sugar
- candy hearts or sprinkles for decorating

Instructions

1. Warm the oven to 350° Fahrenheit and line an 8x8" pan one way with parchment paper.
2. In the mini stand mixer bowl fitted with the paddle attachment, make the cookies: put the softened butter and mix on medium-high speed for about thirty seconds to fluff it up. Gently put in the granulated sugar while continuing to beat.
3. After that, put the egg and vanilla extract and beat to combine.
4. Turn the stand blender off and evenly distribute the baking powder, flour, and salt on top.
5. To incorporate the dry ingredients, turn the blender back to LOW and beat.
6. Scoop the batter into the cooking pan and press it down with your fingers.
7. Bake for twenty minutes, or until a toothpick introduced comes out mostly clean with only a few crumbs. Let cool completely.
8. In a clean mini-stand blender bowl, make the frosting: blend the cream cheese and softened butter for one minute until fluffy. Add the vanilla and beat until combined.
9. Turn the blender to low and gradually add the powdered sugar, one-half cup at a time, while mixing.
10. If you feel that it needs to be thinner, then add a splash of milk.
11. Sprinkle the frosting over the cooled cookie, decorate it with candy, and then slice and serve.

72. SMALL BATCH BLONDIES

Prep Time: 10 Mins

Bake Time: 27 Mins

Total Time: 37 Mins

Servings: 8

Ingredients

- 6 tbsp regular or vegan melted butter
- ½ cup of light brown sugar
- ¼ cup of granulated sugar
- 1 egg
- ½ tbsp vanilla extract
- ¼ tsp salt
- ¾ cup + 2 tbsp all-purpose flour

- ⅓ cup of semisweet chocolate chips (regular or vegan)

Instructions

1. Make an 8x4 or 9x5 loaf baking pan with parchment paper, allowing some over the sides to make it easy to take the blondies from the pan. Warm the oven to 350°F.
2. Put the butter in a microwave-safe bowl and warm in the microwave until melted (or melt butter over the stove). Add in both sugars and stir until the combination pulls away easily from the sides of the bowl as you blend, with a paste-like consistency.
3. Stir in the egg and vanilla extract.
4. Add flour and salt, then stir until it's just mixed. Whisk in the chocolate chips.
5. Bake the batter for twenty-six to thirty-six minutes after pouring it into the pan lined with parchment paper and spreading it out in an even layer.
6. The top should be cracked, and a toothpick inserted in the center should come out with only a few wet crumbs, but not completely clean or covered in batter. The batter should also not jiggle in the pan. Let the blondies cool thoroughly in the pan prior to slicing.

73. SERIOUSLY FUDGY SMALL BATCH BROWNIES

Prep Time: 25 Mins

Cook Time: 25 Mins

Total Time: 50 Mins

Servings: 8

Ingredients

- 115 g unsalted butter
- 60 g chopped dark chocolate (70% cacao)
- 3 tbsp cocoa powder
- 1 tsp espresso powder
- 75 g granulated sugar
- 55 g dark brown sugar
- 1 tsp vanilla extract
- ½ tsp fine sea salt
- 2 large eggs
- 45 g all-purpose flour

Instructions

1. Set oven temperature to 350°F, or 180°C. With an overhang on the sides, line a 9 by 5-inch pan with parchment paper. Set aside the parchment paper after greasing it with nonstick cooking spray or butter.
2. Combine the chopped chocolate, espresso powder, and cocoa powder in a small heatproof bowl; set aside.
3. Stirring frequently, cook the butter in a small saucepan over medium flame until it reaches a vigorous simmer. Put the hot butter over the chocolate combination and let it sit for two minutes. Stir the chocolate until it is fully smooth and melted, then set aside.
4. Using an electric hand blender, stir together the salt, brown sugar, granulated sugar, vanilla extract, and eggs for exactly five minutes on high.
5. Put the slightly cooled chocolate combination into the blender and mix for about 2 minutes or until smooth.
6. Add the flour and slowly fold it in with a rubber spatula until well-mixed.
7. Put the batter into the prepared cooking pan and smooth the top with a spatula. Bake for twenty minutes, then take them from the oven and slam them on a flat surface for two to three times to deflate them a little (this gives them an additional even texture and encourages the lovely crackly top). Take the brownies to the oven and bake for an additional five minutes, or until a wooden skewer introduced into the middle comes out fudgy, but the edges seem cooked through. The brownies' middle will appear under baked, but they will continue to cook and set as they chill.
8. If desired, distribute flaky sea salt over the top of the brownies and let them cool completely in the pan. To take the cooled brownies from the pan, use parchment paper; cut into eight bars and enjoy.

74. SMALL-BATCH MONSTER COOKIE BARS

Prep Time: 10 Mins

Cook Time: 15 Mins

Cool Time: 45 Mins

Total Time: 1 Hr 11 Mins

Servings: 6-8

Ingredients

- 3 tbsp salted softened butter (see note)
- ½ cup of peanut butter creamy or chunky (see note)
- ⅓ cup of granulated sugar
- ⅓ cup of brown sugar
- 1 large egg
- ½ tsp vanilla extract
- 1½ cups of quick/instant oats (see note)
- ½ tsp baking soda
- ½ cup of M&M's plus more for topping
- ⅓ cup of chocolate chips

Instructions

1. Warm the oven to 350°F. Grease the loaf pan lightly and line it with parchment paper.
2. In a medium bowl, mix softened butter, peanut butter, and granulated and brown sugars. Beat for approximately a minute or until well combined and a little lighter in color.
3. Put the egg and vanilla and mix until well combined.
4. Distribute oats and baking soda over the top. Mix until well mixed.
5. Combine the M&Ms and chocolate chips with a wooden spoon or spatula.
6. Move the combination to the prepared baking pan and press it out into an even layer. Distribute a few extra M&Ms on top if desired, and bake for approximately fifteen to eighteen minutes or until the edges are lightly browned. Don't overbake!
7. Let the bars to chill in the pan for about forty-five minutes to firm up prior to moving to a cutting board and cutting.
8. Serve and enjoy!

Notes

1. Keep bars at room temperature in an airtight container for three to four days, or freeze in a frozen bag for up to 2 months.
2. Add the baking soda, oats, and ⅛ tsp of salt if you're using unsalted butter.
3. These bars have not been tried with natural peanut butter.
4. You may also use rolled or old-fashioned oats.

75. SMALL BATCH JAM CRUMBLE BARS

Total Time: 20 Mins

Servings: 2

Ingredients

- 95 g granulated sugar
- 210 g plain flour
- ½ tsp baking powder
- ½ tsp salt
- 120 g cold butter, cut into cubes
- 1 large lightly beaten free-range egg
- 160 g your favorite fruit jam
- icing sugar to dust

Instructions

1. Set the oven's temperature to 190°C (375°F) or gas mark 5. Butter and line a 9 by 5-inch loaf tin with baking paper. Set aside.
2. In a bowl, sieve flour and baking powder. Combine the salt and sugar. Put the butter and blend it in with a pastry cutter until the combination looks like fine bread crumbs. With a fork, whisk in the beaten egg. Once pressed together, the dough should be dry and crumbly but still form a dough.
3. Take 100 g for the topping and press the remaining dough into the prepared pan. Spoon the jam on top and distribute evenly. Sprinkle the reserved dough evenly over the top.
4. Bake in the heated oven for forty to forty-five minutes or until golden brown and the edges begin to come away from the pan sides. Let it chill thoroughly on a wire rack.
5. Dust with icing sugar and sliced into squares prior to serving. These delicious bars can be kept in an airtight container for up to one week.

76. MINI-BATCH SNICKERS BARS

Prep Time: 5 Mins

Freeze Time: 1 Hr

Total Time: 1 Hr 5 Mins

Servings: 4

Ingredients

Nougat Layer

- 1 tbsp peanut butter
- 1 tbsp maple syrup
- ¼ cup of oat flour

Caramel Nut Layer

- 2 tsp coconut oil
- 2 tsp peanut butter
- 2 tsp maple syrup
- 3 tbsp peanuts

Chocolate Coating

- ⅓ cup of chocolate chips
- 1 tsp coconut oil

Instructions

1. To make a non-sticky dough, combine peanut butter, oat flour, and maple syrup in a bowl.
2. Press into a rectangle (or use muffin cups). You may use some parchment. This layer is your nougat.
3. Melt the peanut butter, coconut oil, and maple syrup in the microwave to make the caramel nut layer. Whisk in the peanuts.
4. Sprinkle the mix over the nougat layer. Freeze until solid (1 hour at least).
5. Whisk the chocolate and coconut oil in the microwave for thirty seconds at a time or until the chocolate is completely melted.
6. Take the frozen bars and cut them into four.
7. Dip each frozen piece in chocolate using one or two forks, then place it on a piece of parchment. To set the chocolate, refrigerate or refreeze.
8. Store frozen or refrigerated, and enjoy!

77. MONSTER COOKIE BARS

Prep Time: 10 Mins

Cook Time: 30 Mins

Total Time: 40 Mins

Servings: 24

Ingredients

- 2 cups of spooned and leveled all-purpose flour
- 2 cups of old-fashioned oats
- 1 tsp baking soda
- 1 tsp sea salt
- 1 cup of unsalted butter at room temperature
- 1 cup of creamy peanut butter
- 1½ cups of packed light brown sugar
- ½ cup of granulated sugar
- 2 large eggs
- 1 tbsp vanilla extract
- 1¼ cups of semi-sweet chocolate chips
- 1½ cups of divided M&M'S
- flaky sea salt for sprinkling on bars

Instructions

1. Warm the oven to 350 degrees F. Use a lot of nonstick cooking spray to grease a 9x13-inch pan.
2. In a big bowl, stir together the flour, oats, baking soda, and salt. Set aside.
3. In the stand blender bowl, cream the butter, peanut butter, and sugars together until smooth, for approximately two minutes, scraping down the side of the bowl with a spatula, if necessary. Mix in the eggs and vanilla until well-mixed.
4. Add the dried ingredients and blend until just mixed; don't over-mix.
5. Whisk in the chocolate chips and 1 cup of M&Ms.
6. Sprinkle the combination evenly into the prepared pan with a spatula. Top with the remaining ½ cup of M&Ms.
7. Bake for twenty-five to thirty-five minutes or until the bars are lightly golden brown and set. Do not overbake. You do not want the bars to be dry. Take the pan from the oven and distribute it with flaky sea salt. In the pan, let the bars cool. Once cool, cut into bars and serve.

78. GRAIN-FREE AND SUGAR-FREE MAGIC COOKIE BARS

Prep Time: 10 Mins

Cook Time: 25 Mins

Total Time: 35 Mins

Servings: 12-15

Ingredients

- 1½ cups of almond meal
- ½ cup of dairy-free butter
- 8 to 14 Ounces sweetened condensed milk
- 1⅓ cups of coconut flakes (finely shredded, no sugar added)
- 1 cup of chopped pecans
- 1⅔ cups of chocolate chips (dairy-free, soy-free, sugar-free, and homemade chips work well)

Instructions

Make the Sweetened Condensed Milk

1. Put the coconut milk and Truvia in a small pan and bring to a light boil.
2. Increase the flame to maintain a steady simmer for approximately four hours. To prevent burning, whisk occasionally.
3. It is done when reduced by approximately half and thick in consistency, like store-bought sweetened condensed milk.

Make the Bars

4. Warm the oven to 350 degrees.
5. In a blender or with a fork, mix almond meal with butter.
6. Use a well-greased 9-by-13-inch Pyrex dish to press the almond meal combination into it.
7. Top the almond mixture with the sweetened condensed milk.
8. Sprinkle the coconut and chocolate chips evenly over the sweetened condensed milk.
9. Use a fork to press down evenly.
10. Alternatively, add half of the sweetened condensed milk first, followed by the coconut and chocolate chips, then the remaining sweetened condensed milk on top.
11. It works well either way.

12. Bake at 350 degrees for approximately twenty-five minutes or until bubbly and brown.
13. Cool well.
14. You could even keep it in the refrigerator overnight.
15. Slice, serve, and enjoy!

79. HEALTHY PUMPKIN CHOCOLATE CHIP OAT BARS (VEGAN AND GLUTEN FREE)

Prep Time: 10 Mins

Cook Time: 20 Mins

Total Time: 30 Mins

Servings: 16

Ingredients

- 3 cups of gluten-free oats
- 1 tsp baking powder
- ¼ tsp salt
- 1 ½ tsp cinnamon
- ¼ tsp nutmeg
- ⅛ tsp ground cloves or allspice
- 2 tsp pure vanilla extract
- 1 cup of canned pumpkin
- ½ cup of unsweetened applesauce
- ½ cup of packed dark brown sugar
- 1 tbsp olive or melted coconut oil
- ⅓ cup of vegan chocolate chips, plus two tbsp for sprinkling on top

Instructions

1. Warm the oven to 350 degrees F. Sprinkle a 9x9-inch cooking pan with nonstick cooking spray.
2. Make oat flour: Put oatmeal into a blender and blend for one to two minutes until oatmeal resembles flour. You may need to stop the blender and stir the oats a few times to ensure that all of them are blended.
3. Take out 2½ cups of the oat flour and put it in a medium-sized bowl. Stir in baking powder, salt, and spices; set aside.

4. In a separate big bowl, stir together the pumpkin, oil, brown sugar, vanilla extract, and applesauce for one to two minutes until smooth and creamy.
5. Gently add in the oat flour combination and mix until just combined.
6. Add ⅓ cup of chocolate chips and gently fold. Put the batter into the prepared pan and top with the remaining two tbsp of chocolate chips.
7. Bake for fifteen to twenty-five minutes, or until a knife introduced in the middle comes out clean or with a few crumbs attached. Check after about fifteen minutes, but the exact time will depend on the size of the pan you use. When finished baking, cool for ten minutes on a wire rack. Cut into sixteen slices.

(PIES, TARTS, AND QUICHE RECIPES)

80. SMALL BATCH PUMPKIN PIE

Prep Time: 1 Hr

Cook Time: 55 Mins

Total Time: 1 Hr 55 Mins

Servings: 6

Ingredients

- 1 perfect pie crust recipe
- 3 medium eggs
- ¾ cup plus 1 tbsp pumpkin purée
- 1½ tsp pure vanilla extract
- 2 tbsp golden brown sugar
- 2 tsp cornstarch or arrowroot starch
- ¾ tsp cinnamon
- ½ tsp ground ginger
- ¼ tsp ground nutmeg
- ¼ tsp ground allspice
- ⅛ tsp ground cloves
- ½ tsp kosher salt
- 6 tsp pure maple syrup
- ¾ cup of heavy 35%-40% cream
- Egg wash (one egg combined with a little water)
- 1-2 tbsp raw or turbinado sugar
- 1 tsp Maldon Sea salt for finishing (optional)
- sweetened whipped cream for garnish it can be plain if you'd rather!

Instructions

1. Set the oven's temperature to 375 °F, or 190 °C.
2. Roll out ½ of the pie pastry and line a removable bottom pie plate or tart pan (6-7 or 8 inches). The amount of filling that can fit in the pan is determined by its depth. As desired, trim or crimp. In the freezer until the filling is ready.

3. Roll out the remaining ½ of the pie pastry to a thickness of approximately ⅙ inch, similar to your pie crust. Cut out the shapes in the desired shapes (don't cut out as many as you need because some might brown too much in the oven). Put these on a baking sheet lined with parchment and refrigerate until needed.
4. In a big bowl, stir the eggs till frothy.
5. Blend in the pumpkin purée and vanilla until completely combined.
6. In a small bowl, stir together the sugar, starch, spices, and salt. Combine this with the squash combination.
7. Add the maple syrup. Stir well. Finally, whisk in the cream.
8. Put the chilled pie shell on a baking sheet. Run a little egg wash along the edges of your crimped pie shell. Distribute the edges with a little of your raw or turbinado sugar.
9. Put the filling into the pie shell. If there is any leftover, fill a ramekin dish with it and bake it alongside the pie until it is set.
10. Bake on the center rack. Bake for 45–55 minutes, rotating the pie after approximately thirty minutes to ensure even browning of the crust. Check at forty-five minutes, depending on the size of the pie plate or tart pan you're using. You also never know what your oven is like.
11. The pie is ready when the edges of the filling puff up, and the center of the pie jiggles a little when the baking sheet is moved.
12. Cool on a wire rack.
13. While the pie is baking, take out the chilled 'cookies' from the fridge.
14. Massage each with egg wash and then distribute with raw or turbinado sugar.
15. Bake at 375 degrees F till golden, approximately fifteen to twenty minutes. Take it and let it cool on a rack for approximately thirty minutes.
16. Put the cooled cookies in an appealing pattern on top of the cooled custard.
17. When the pie is at room temperature, you can wrap it loosely with plastic cover and keep in the freezer till ready to serve. Best served slightly cold.

81. SMALL PIE CRUST (6 INCH PIE PAN)

Prep Time: 30 Mins

Cook Time: 20 Mins

Chill Time: 1 Hr 30 Mins

Total Time: 2 Hrs 20 Mins

Servings: 4-6

Ingredients

- 1 cup of all-purpose flour
- 2 tbsp granulated sugar (optional, can leave out for savory pies)
- ½ tsp salt
- 3 tbsp cold shortening (cut into three pieces)
- 3 tbsp cold unsalted butter (cut into three pieces)
- 2 tbsp cold water

Instructions

1. In the bowl of a large food processor, add the sugar, flour, and salt. Pulse one time to combine.
2. To make it by hand, add it to a big mixing bowl.
3. Combine the cold butter and cold shortening. Pulse until the flour is cut up into small pebbles.
4. If making by hand, cut the fat with a pastry blender or two knives.
5. Add the water and pulse until dough forms. If it appears crumbly, pulse for one additional minute.
6. If it still doesn't come together, add a tsp of water, but don't use too much, or your crust will puff out too much.
7. Use a spoon to stir in the water if making by hand.
8. Move the dough on a piece of plastic wrap and form it into an equally round disk. Top with another piece of plastic wrap and chill for at least an hour.
9. Roll the dough into an 8-inch circle that is between ⅛-¼ inch thick after it has cooled. Roll it out on a lightly floured surface or between the plastic wrap.
10. If your dough is sticking, chill for an additional fifteen minutes or until cold.
11. Move the dough to a 6-inch ungreased glass pie plate, a greased disposable pie plate, a greased springform pan, or a greased cake pan. If you're having trouble, you can put the dough back together in the pan.

12. Trim off any excess dough, then shape the crust as desired. Stick a fork in the bottom and put it in the fridge for at least thirty minutes.
13. Warm the oven to 400°F. Have a baking sheet ready at room temperature.
14. Line the top of the pie crust with greased foil, touching the dough, and then fill with pie weights like dried lentils or beans.
15. Put your pie pan on the room-temperature baking sheet. Bake for fifteen minutes.
16. Don't put a cold pan directly on a hot oven rack or baking sheet. A sudden temperature change may cause your pan to shatter.
17. Take the foil and weights, then bake for an additional five minutes or until the bottom is golden brown and no longer appears uncooked.
18. At this point, double-check the pie recipe. You are done if you are blind baking your crust.
19. If your crust needs further baking, bake for another ten to fifteen minutes or until golden brown and done.
20. Cool the crust while you finish the pie recipe. If you're not filling it right away, let it cool fully, then cover and refrigerate for up to three days or freeze for up to six months.

82. SMALL-BATCH WHOOPIE PIES

Prep Time: 10 Mins

Cook Time: 10 Mins

Assembly Time: 10 Mins

Total Time: 30 Mins

Servings: 7

Ingredients

Brownie Cookie Dough

- 1 tbsp melted coconut oil
- 2 tbsp nut or seed butter
- 3 tbsp maple syrup
- 2 tbsp nut milk
- ½ tsp vanilla extract
- ¼ cup of cocoa powder
- ¼ cup of flour gf all-purpose if desired

- ¼ tsp baking powder
- pinch of salt

Filling

- 2 tbsp vegan softened cream cheese
- ⅓ cup of powder sugar
- drop of vanilla extract

Instructions

1. Mix all of the filling ingredients until light and frothy (with a fork or hand blender). It should have the consistency of frosting; modify with a drop of water or additional powder sugar. Refrigerate.
2. Warm the oven to 350°F and prepare a baking sheet with parchment paper.
3. Blend together the oil, syrup, nut butter, nut milk, and vanilla.
4. Stir together the flour, cocoa, baking powder, and salt.
5. When you combine the two, the dough will be somewhere between cookie dough and brownie batter. If it's too dry, add a drop of milk; if it's too wet, add a pinch of flour.
6. Put the scoop on a baking sheet and bake for ten minutes.
7. Cool the cookies completely prior to assembling the whoopie pies, filling each sandwich with a heaping tsp of frosting.
8. Enjoy your pies! If you used cream cheese for the center, keep them in the fridge.

83. MINI PECAN PIES (MINI MUFFIN PAN)

Prep Time: 2 Hrs 20 Mins

Cook Time: 18 Mins

Total Time: 3 Hrs

Servings: 24

Ingredients

- 1 unbaked pie crust or all butter pie crust
- 3 tbsp unsalted butter
- ½ cup of packed dark brown sugar
- 1 tsp pure vanilla extract
- 1 large egg
- ½ tsp ground cinnamon
- ¼ tsp ground nutmeg
- ¾ cup of chopped pecans
- coarse salt for sprinkling

Instructions

1. **Pie crust:** Before I begin making the mini pies, I like to make sure the pie dough is ready. Make pie dough the night prior to since it has to cool in the refrigerator for at least two hours before use.
2. **Shape the mini crusts:** Put the dough on a floured work surface. Roll into a big 12-inch circle. If necessary, use warm hands to mold any cracked edges back together. Use a 2.75-inch cookie cutter to cut rounds from the circle. You'll have to reroll the dough scraps several times. Work quickly, as the dough gets more fragile the longer it sits at room temperature. You will get approximately twenty-four rounds.
3. Grease a 24-count mini muffin pan. The best spray is nonstick. In a greased muffin pan, place the dough rounds. Up the sides and into the crevice's bottom, press the dough into a flat surface. To help the little crusts set their form, refrigerate the pan for five to ten minutes while the oven preheats.
4. Set oven temperature to 325 degrees F (163°C). When the dough has briefly chilled, pre-bake the crusts for seven minutes. So, the bottom of the crust can be baked properly and not get soggy from the pecan filling. Set the oven's temperature to 350°F (177°C).

5. **For the filling:** To make the filling, warm the butter in a small bowl in the microwave or on the stove. Allow to cool gently for a few minutes. In a medium bowl, stir the cinnamon, nutmeg, vanilla, and brown sugar. Stir in the melted butter, then the pecans.
6. Fill each warm crust with 1-2 tsp of the filling. Top with coarse salt.
7. Bake the filled mini pies for sixteen to eighteen minutes. Be careful not to overbake. When the crust begins to brown a bit, the mini pies are done.
8. Let the tiny pies to completely cool in the pan prior to serving. (A spoon makes it easy to get them out.) Put a dollop of whipped cream on top when serving.
9. Keep leftovers in the refrigerator or at room temperature with a cover for up to three days.

84. MINI PIE CRUST

Prep Time: 10 Mins

Cook Time: 20 Mins

Cool Time: 20 Mins

Total Time: 50 Mins

Serving: 1

Ingredients

Butter Crust

- 5 tbsp all-purpose flour
- 1 tsp granulated sugar
- ⅛ tsp salt
- 2 tbsp cold salted butter
- 2 tsp ice water

Instructions

1. Warm the oven to 400 degrees Fahrenheit, or 200 degrees Celsius.
2. In a small bowl, mix salt, flour, and sugar. Cut the butter into the mixture with a fork until it resembles moist sand.
3. To form dough, add water and stir.
4. Turn the dough out onto a piece of plastic wrap. Flatten into a disc and cover completely with plastic wrap. Put it in the fridge for twenty minutes.

5. When the dough has chilled, unwrap it and put it on a piece of parchment paper. Wrap with a second sheet of parchment paper. Roll the dough into a six-inch round circle, approximately ⅛-inch thick, using a rolling pin.
6. Put the parchment paper and dough on a baking sheet, then remove the top piece of parchment.
7. Add the pie filling and bake for an additional twenty minutes until the crust is golden.

85. MINI PUMPKIN PIES

Total Time: 45 Mins

Serving: 9

Ingredients

- 1 (9-inch) pie crust (homemade or store-bought)
- ½ cup of pumpkin puree
- ¼ cup of condensed milk
- ¼ cup of brown sugar
- 1 tsp pumpkin spice blend
- ¼ tsp salt
- 1 egg
- whipped cream for topping (optional)

Instructions

1. Warm the oven to 375 degrees F.
2. In a big mixing bowl, stir together pumpkin puree, pumpkin spice, condensed milk, brown sugar, and salt. Add the egg and whisk until the combination is smooth and uniform. Set aside.
3. Roll the pie dough into a broad circle about ⅛-inch thick. Cut nine circles with a 3.5-inch round cookie cutter (or the rim of a can of pumpkin puree). Use any leftover pie crust to cut out small pieces for garnish on top.
4. Slowly press each pie dough circle into the cavity of a standard 12-cup muffin pan to fit snugly. It will wrap up to half of the height of each cavity (but will not reach the top). Nine cavities will be filled by you. To ensure a uniform thickness, do not overstretch the pie crust. After that, pleat the crust's edges with a fork.
5. Fill each pie crust with 1.5 tbsp of pumpkin filling, about ¾ of the way up the crust. Do not overfill since the filling will expand while baking. If you have little forms cut from scraps, you may layer them on top.

6. Bake for twenty minutes in a heated oven until the crust is softly golden brown and the pumpkin filling has set. Take the muffin pan from the oven and allow it to cool for at least twenty minutes. The drop-in temperature could cause the pumpkin filling to crack. To avoid this, turn off the oven and leave the muffin tin inside for another thirty minutes to allow the pies to cool gently and without breaking.
7. Serve the little pumpkin pies, either cold or warm. Top the small pumpkin pies with whipped cream and a sprinkling of pumpkin spice mix or cinnamon.

86. APPLE PIE FROM SCRATCH

Prep Time: 20 Mins

Cook Time: 40 Mins

Additional Time: 30 Mins

Total Time: 1 Hr 30 Mins

Serving: 6

Ingredients

- 1 cup of unbleached flour
- ¼ tsp salt
- 2 ounces diced cold unsalted butter
- ¼ tsp apple cider vinegar
- 3-4 tbsp cold water

For the Filling

- 2 medium Honeycrisp apples
- ¾ tsp orange zest
- ⅛ tsp allspice
- ¼ tsp cinnamon
- ¼ cup of sugar
- 2 tsp milk for brushing on the crust
- coarse sugar for sprinkling on the crust (optional)

Instructions

1. First, prepare the crust by whisking together the flour and salt in a medium bowl.
2. Toss in the cold, diced butter using two knives or a pastry cutter. Once the butter is about the size of peas, squeeze the dough between your hands. In a few minutes, the dough will come together with the aid of your warm hands. Put the bowl in the refrigerator for approximately ten minutes or until the dough forms a clump when squeezed between your hands.
3. Take the flour mix out of the fridge after ten minutes and add the apple cider vinegar and two tbsp of ice water. Mix this combination with a fork until it comes together. As needed, add extra water. Do not add more than five tbsp of water.
4. Shape the dough into a flat disk, cover in plastic, and refrigerate for thirty minutes.
5. Warm the oven to 425°F and prepare a 6-7-inch metal pie tin.
6. Peel and sliced the apples into thin slices. Cut the apple slices in half so that they are approximately 2-inch-long. Toss the apples in a bowl with the orange zest, cinnamon, allspice, and sugar. As you roll out the crust, let it set.
7. Divide the dough in half on a slightly floured board, leaving a little extra for the bottom crust. Roll the bottom crust into a circle that is one inch larger than the diameter of the pie pan. Wrap the crust over the pie tin and carefully fit it up the sides; don't strain the dough.
8. Now, roll the top into a 7-inch circle. Have it ready on the side. Put the apple filling into the bottom crust, pressing firmly to eliminate any air gaps. Slowly lay the top crust over the apples. Cut two slits in the middle of the crust for ventilation, and prettily pin the seams together. Massage the pie lightly with milk and distribute with sugar on top.
9. Bake for twenty minutes on the lowest oven rack. Increase the oven temperature to 350°F and move the pie to the middle rack to keep baking for another fifteen to twenty minutes until the filling is bubbling. Let cool for at least two hours prior to serving.

87. EASY MINI APPLE PIES

Total Time: 38 Mins

Serving: 12

Ingredients

Crust

- 2 cups of flour
- ⅔ cup of chilled butter
- 1 tsp salt
- 4 tbsp water

Filling

- 5 medium apples (peeled & chopped up into small pieces)
- ¾ cup of sugar
- 2 tsp cinnamon
- 6 tbsp flour
- 2 tbsp chilled butter

Directions

1. Warm the oven to 425 degrees. Get out the muffin pan. There's no need to grease it.
2. In a blender, blend flour, salt, and butter until it looks like little peas.
3. Add water and mix just until it appears to be sticking.
4. Take it out and mix it by hand until well blended.
5. To make it about ¼ inch thick, roll it out on a lightly floured surface.
6. Cut twelve 4-inch circles with a bowl or cup. (You'll need to roll it out twice).
7. Note: You can do anything you want with the rest of the crust on top of the pies.
8. To form small bowls, press each circle into muffin tins until it is all the way up each side.
9. Mix all of the filling ingredients by hand and spoon them into muffin bowls.
10. Cut up butter into twelve tiny pieces and place one piece on each pie.
11. You may decorate them whatever you like with additional crust, or keep them plain.
12. Bake at 425 degrees for sixteen to eighteen minutes. (Until the crust turns light brown and the apples bubble).
13. Once cool, just loosen them with a spoon, and they'll come right out!

88. APPLE HAND PIES

Prep Time: 20 Mins

Cook Time: 15 Mins

Total Time: 35 Mins

Serving: 4

Ingredients

- half a premade pie crust 9-inch (thawed as directed on the package)
- half a medium granny smith apple (cored & chopped into small ¼-inch pieces)
- 1 tbsp roughly chopped dried cranberries
- 1 tbsp roughly chopped pecans pieces
- 1 tbsp brown sugar
- ⅛ tsp ground cinnamon
- ¼ tsp cornstarch
- 2 tbsp unsweetened applesauce
- 2 tsp heavy cream
- granulated sugar for topping

Instructions

1. Warm your oven to 400°F (375°F for convection/forced fan ovens) with the cooking rack in the middle position. Choose the BAKE setting on a toaster oven.
2. Grease a quarter sheet pan lightly or line it with a silicone baking mat.
3. Combine the apple, cranberries, pecans, brown sugar, cinnamon, and cornstarch until well coated. Whisk in the applesauce. Taste and add extra sugar or spices if desired.
4. Split the pie crust into four equal pieces and form them into balls.
5. Put a ball of dough on a surface dusted with flour or parchment paper.
6. Simply roll it into a circle approximately five inches across. Repeat the process with the remaining dough.
7. On one side of each round, spoon a quarter of the filling. Use water to moisten the dough's edges. Then, fold the untopped dough over the filled side and use a fork to secure the edges.
8. Move the pies to your prepared pan.
9. To release steam during baking, cut three tiny vents into the top of each pie.
10. Massage the pie dough lightly with half-and-half or cream, then distribute with sugar if desired.
11. In about fourteen to sixteen minutes, or until golden brown, bake.

12. To cool completely, move baked pies to a wire rack.
13. Enjoy pies warm or at room temp; they go well with vanilla ice cream!

89. PECAN BUTTER TARTS

Total Time: 1 Hr

Serving: 6

Ingredients

For the Pastry

- 1 cup plus two tbsp plain all-purpose flour
- 1 tbsp sugar
- ¼ tsp salt
- ½ cup of cold butter (cut into bits)
- 3 tbsp cold water
- ½ tbsp lemon juice or white vinegar

For the Filling

- 1 large free-range egg
- 3 tbsp butter
- ½ cup of dark brown or demerara sugar
- ¼ cup of pure maple syrup
- ½ tbsp lemon juice
- ½ tsp vanilla extract
- pinch salt
- 1 cup of toasted pecans

Instructions

1. Make the pastry first. In a bowl, whisk flour, sugar, and salt. Drop in the butter and sliced it in until the combination resembles coarse crumbs using a pastry blender or two round bladed knives.
2. Whisk together the lemon juice and water. Add this to the dry combination all at once, just mixing until the dough comes together. Shape into a six-inch long log. Put it in the fridge for at least two hours afterward. Take from the refrigerator approximately half an hour prior to you intend to bake the tarts.
3. Once you are ready to bake the tarts, warm the oven to 400° Fahrenheit/200°C/gas mark. 6. Grease a six-cup muffin tin very lightly.

4. Cut the pastry lump into six pieces. Roll each piece into a four ½-inch circle on a lightly floured surface. Use to line the muffin cup holes, making sure they go ½ inch above the holes in the tin. Put in the refrigerator to cool while you prepare the filling.
5. In a saucepan, heat the brown sugar and butter over medium flame until the mixture begins to boil. Take from the flame.
6. In a bowl, stir the egg with the salt, vanilla, lemon juice, and maple syrup. Gently stir in the sugar and butter combination, stirring constantly and taking care not to scramble the egg.
7. Split the toasted pecans between the pastry shells. Using a ladle spoon, evenly distribute the filling over the nuts.
8. Bake the tarts at 400°F/200°C/gas mark six for ten minutes. Increase the oven temperature to 375° Fahrenheit (190°C) (gas mark 5). Bake for another ten to fifteen minutes or until the filling bubbles and the crust edges brown.
9. Cool the tarts in the tin for about four minutes, then carefully flip them around in the pan to avoid sticking. Keep them in the pan until fully cooled.
10. These are best served at room temp. Do keep any leftovers in the refrigerator.

90. MINI FRUIT TARTS WITH VANILLA PASTRY CREAM

Prep Time: 45 Mins

Cook Time: 45 Mins

Chill Time: 3 Hrs

Total Time: 4 Hrs 30 Mins

Serving: 6

Ingredients

Mini-Tart Crust

- 1½ cups of unbleached flour
- ⅓ cup of powdered sugar
- ¼ tsp salt
- ½ cup of chilled unsalted butter
- 1 egg yolk
- 1 tbsp heavy cream

Cream Filling

- 2¾ cups of milk
- ⅔ cup of sugar
- ¼ cup of cornstarch
- ⅛ tsp salt
- 4 egg yolks
- 2 tbsp unsalted butter
- 1 tsp vanilla extract

Glaze

- ¼ cup of currant jelly

Instructions

Crust

1. In a food processor, combine 1½ cups of unbleached flour, ⅓ cup of powdered sugar, and ¼ tsp salt.
2. Cut ½ cup of unsalted butter into eight slices and add to the flour combination, pulsing several times until the combination resembles oatmeal. Combine one egg yolk with one tbsp heavy cream.
3. Pulse until all the ingredients are moistened. Let the machine run for a few seconds until the dough begins to cling together. (If the dough appears too dried, add a few extra drops of cream.)
4. As with refrigerated cookie dough, press the dough into a roll. Wrap tightly in plastic and refrigerate for thirty minutes.
5. Sprinkle the molds generously with Baker's Secret or something similar. (Baker's Secret is an aerosol spray that combines flour and oil.) Greasing is unnecessary when using silicone molds.
6. Cut the dough roll into twelve equal pieces. Roll the dough between two parts of plastic wrap into a circle that is slightly bigger than the tart moulds. Press into a mold with your fingers, being careful to keep the thickness consistent. Cut off any extra at the top with a knife. Freeze for at least thirty minutes, overnight, or for up to one month.
7. Put the frozen tart shells on a cookie sheet. Shape each small square of foil to fit the shape of the crust by pressing it down.
8. Bake at 400°F (200°C) for ten minutes. Take the foil and bake until golden brown, approximately three to four minutes.

Cream Filling

9. To a blender bowl, add 2¾ cups of milk, ⅔ cup of sugar, ¼ cup of cornstarch, ⅛ tsp salt, and four egg yolks. (If you only have a bowl and a whisk, you can do it with that.)
10. Blend for five seconds, then pour into a 2-quart glass microwave-safe bowl.
11. Microwave for six to seven minutes on HIGH, whisking after three minutes and again every minute after that. (If it's still not thick after seven minutes, keep microwaving.)
12. Whisk in 2 tbsp unsalted butter and one tsp vanilla extract until completely smooth.
13. If the heated custard is not ready to assemble, cover it with plastic wrap and smooth it to the surface. This prevents skin from developing on top of the cream.

Assembly

14. Put cream filling in each baked tart shell. Top with your preferred fruit.

Glaze

15. Warm ¼ cup of currant jelly in the microwave or on the flame, then use a brush to apply the shininess on each piece of fruit. It's okay if some spills on the cream.

---

91. TINY PECAN TARTS

Prep Time: 30 Mins

Cook Time: 30 Mins

Total Time: 1 Hr

Serving: 24

Ingredients

Pastry

- 1 cup of butter
- 6 ounces softened cream cheese
- 2 cups of all-purpose flour

Filling

- 4 large eggs
- 3 cups of packed brown sugar

- 1 cup of chopped pecans
- 4 tbsp melted butter
- 1 tsp vanilla extract
- 1 pinch salt

Directions

1. Set the oven's temperature to 350° Fahrenheit (175 degrees Celsius). Lightly grease two tiny tart pans.
2. **Make the pastry:** In a large bowl, combine butter and cream cheese; beat with an electric mixer until smooth and creamy. Put the flour and mix until the dough is smooth.
3. Split the dough into forty-eight balls and place one in each of the greased tart pans. Use your fingers or a tart tamper and press out into a tart shell.
4. **Make the filling:** Break the eggs into a big bowl. Combine brown sugar, pecans, melted butter, vanilla, and salt; mix well. Fill each ¾ full of prepared tart shells with filling.
5. Bake in the heated oven for approximately thirty minutes or until golden. To cool completely, move the tarts to a wire rack.

92. MINIATURE BAKEWELL TARTS

Prep Time: 15 Mins

Cook Time: 30 Mins

Resting Time: 30 Mins

Total Time: 1 Hr 15 Mins

Serving: 6

Ingredients

Pastry

- 50 g flour
- 25 g butter
- 1 tsp sugar
- pinch of salt
- 2.5 tsp ice water

Almond Frangipane & Raspberry Jam Filling

- 60 g softened butter
- 60 g sugar
- ¼ tsp almond extract
- 1 egg yolk
- 60 g ground almonds or almond flour
- raspberry jam

Instructions

Make the Pastry

1. In a medium bowl, mix salt, flour, and sugar. Rub the cold butter into the flour until the combination looks like bread crumbs.
2. Whisk in the cold water, then gently knead the dough into a ball use your hands. Cover with clingfilm and refrigerate for approximately thirty minutes.

Make the Almond Filling

3. Cream the butter and sugar together, and then whisk in the almond extract and egg yolk until smooth. When smooth, mix in the ground almonds or almond flour. Let it to rest in the refrigerator while you bake the pastry.

Roll and Bake the Pastry

4. Warm the oven to 350 °F.
5. Roll out the pastry and cut little rounds that will fit well into your tiny muffin tray. If you re-roll the pastry once or twice, you should be able to make five miniature tarts out of it.
6. Use a fork to make holes in the bottom of each tart, then chill for fifteen minutes.
7. After the pastry has rested, bake it for ten minutes. After ten minutes, press on the pastry with a spoon to deflate any puffed-up areas. Return the pastry to the oven for another five to ten minutes until golden brown.

Fill and Bake the Tarts

8. Fill each tart with a small spoon of jam, then fill the rest with almond frangipane.
9. Bake at 325°F for twelve to fifteen minutes or until the tops are very lightly golden brown.

Notes

1. You can store the extra frangipane in the fridge for up to a week or in the freezer for up to three months.

93. MINI TART SHELLS RECIPE

Prep Time: 20 Mins

Cook Time: 14 Mins

Chill Time: 2 Hrs

Total Time: 34 Mins

Serving: 22

Ingredients
Tart Shells Cookie Dough

- 3 cups of all-purpose flour
- ⅛ tsp salt
- 1¼ cups of powdered sugar
- 3 egg yolks
- 2 tsp vanilla bean paste
- 2 sticks unsalted butter at room temperature

Instructions
Tart Shell Dough Recipe

1. Sift ⅛ tsp salt and 3 cups of flour. Set aside.
2. Mix two sticks (226 grams) of unsalted room-temperature butter and 1 cup and ¼ cup of powdered sugar in a mixer attachment with petals until smooth. In a small dish, stir together egg yolks (three egg yolks) and vanilla bean paste or vanilla extract (2 tsp). Gradually combine the egg yolk mixture with the creamed butter. If you need to, scrape the bowl a few times.
3. Put the flour combination to the butter combination gradually on low speed. Mix until it begins to come together. If the dough is too crumbly, add one tsp milk. Don't overwork the dough. To make a ball with your hands, turn the dough over onto a clean surface or into a large bowl. Next, shape the dough into a disk, wrap it in foil, and refrigerate for 1 to 2 hours.

Shape and Bake Mini Tart Shells

4. Warm the oven to 350 °F.
5. Put the mini tart shell molds on a baking sheet. Sprinkle with a non-stick spray and put aside.
6. Take out the chilled dough and sliced it in half. Let it soften for five minutes. Roll it out between two sheets of parchment or use a Dough EZ Mat. Using a ⅛-inch thickness, roll it out.
7. Get rid of as many rounds as you can. Gather scraps and reroll. Use a fork to pierce the shells' bottom. Chill the unbaked tarts for fifteen minutes.
8. Bake at 350 degrees Fahrenheit for twelve to fourteen minutes or until golden around the edges.
9. Let the tarts cool for ten to fifteen minutes prior to removing them from the molds. To release the shell, turn the mold upside down and forcefully tap it down on your work area.
10. Let the tarts cool prior to filling.

94. MINI QUICHE RECIPE

Prep Time: 5 Mins

Cook Time: 15 Mins

Total Time: 20 Mins

Serving: 48

Ingredients

- 1 pie crust recipe (optional)
- 6 large beaten eggs
- 1 cup of heavy cream
- salt and pepper
- pinch cayenne pepper
- 1½ cups of grated cheddar cheese

Optional Add-ins

- chopped spinach
- chopped broccoli
- cleaned and diced mushrooms
- diced onion

- minced garlic
- cooked and crumbled bacon
- cooked and chopped seafood

Instructions

1. Warm the oven to 375º F.
2. Set aside the mini muffin tin and spray it with nonstick cooking spray.
3. Cut the pie crust with a tiny round cutter, insert it in the muffin tin's indentations, and bake for about fifteen minutes. You can also put each of the pre-made phyllo cups into the muffin tin. Simply omit the crust to make a crustless mini quiche.
4. To make the eggs light and fluffy, whisk them with heavy cream or half-and-half. Combine the salt, pepper, and cayenne pepper until thoroughly mixed. Whisk in cheese. Put into pie shells and top with add-in options as desired. Bake the egg combination for fifteen to twenty-five minutes or until set. Take from the oven and allow it to rest for five minutes prior to serving.
5. Serve warm.

95. CRUSTLESS QUICHE

Prep Time: 15 Mins

Cook Time: 15 Mins

Total Time: 30 Mins

Serving: 12

Ingredients

- 6 eggs
- 3 tbsp milk
- ½ tsp mixed herbs
- ¼ tsp salt
- ¼ tsp pepper
- ½ cup of chopped cooked bacon, shredded chicken
- 1 cup of cheese
- optional additions, finely chopped: capsicum, onions, broccoli, tomato, spring onions, grated carrot, corn, etc.

Instructions

1. Warm the oven to 180C.
2. Sprinkle the muffin tray thoroughly with cooking oil.
3. Grate the cheese, fry the bacon and dice if using, and finely dice any veggies you use before setting away.
4. In a medium bowl, put the eggs and milk and stir well
5. Stir in the mixed herbs, salt, and pepper.
6. Combine the bacon, cheese, and other vegetables.
7. Spoon onto the prepared muffin tray.
8. Bake for fifteen to eighteen minutes or until they bounce back to the touch.
9. In the muffin tin, let them cool, then carefully take them out.
10. If freezing, let to cool completely prior to freezing.

96. CHOCOLATE CHIP COOKIE RECIPE

Prep Time: 10 Mins

Cook Time: 8 Mins

Total Time: 18 Mins

Serving: 1 Dozen

Ingredients

- 6 tbsp unsalted softened butter
- ¼ cup of dark brown sugar
- 3 tbsp granulated sugar
- 1 large egg yolk
- ¾ tsp vanilla extract
- ½ cup + 2 tbsp all-purpose flour
- ⅛ tsp fine salt
- ¼ tsp baking soda
- ¼ tsp baking powder
- ⅓ cup of chocolate chips

Instructions

1. Warm the oven to 375 degrees. With a silicone mat, line a light-colored baking sheet.
2. In a medium bowl, blend butter with an electric blender on medium speed until fluffy, approximately twenty seconds.

3. Add the sugars and beat for approximately thirty seconds. The combination will turn a pale color and be fluffy.
4. Then, put the egg yolk and vanilla and beat until it's just combined.
5. In a separate bowl, stir baking soda, flour, salt, and baking powder.
6. Distribute the flour on top of the butter combination, and beat just until mixed.
7. Whisk in the chocolate chips.
8. Scoop the dough into twelve dough balls and space them evenly on the baking sheet.
9. Bake for approximately eight to ten minutes, removing the cookies from the oven once the edges begin to turn golden brown.
10. Allow the cookies to rest on the cooking sheet for one minute prior to moving them to a wire rack to cool.

97. SPAGHETTI PIE

Prep Time: 15 Mins

Cook Time: 45 Mins

Total Time: 1 Hr

Serving: 6

Ingredients

- 12 ounces thin spaghetti
- 1-pound lean ground beef
- 1 small diced white or yellow onion
- 1 finely minced garlic clove
- 1 tsp salt
- ½ tsp black pepper
- 1 (28 Ounces) can crushed tomatoes
- 1 (16 Ounces) can tomato sauce
- 1 tsp dried basil
- ½ tsp dried oregano
- 4 ounces softened light cream cheese
- ½ cup of low-fat cottage cheese
- ¾ cup of divided parmesan cheese
- ¾ cup of divided mozzarella cheese

Instructions

1. Sprinkle a deep 9- or 10-inch pie plate lightly with cooking spray and put it aside. Warm the oven to 400 degrees Fahrenheit.
2. Cook the noodles in a big boiling pot, salted water until al dente, following the package directions. While the noodles are boiling, heat a big 12-inch skillet over a medium-high flame and put the ground beef or turkey, breaking it up with a wooden spoon. Add the salt, pepper, onion, and garlic. Cook for approximately five to seven minutes, stirring constantly and continuing to break up the meat, or until it is thoroughly cooked. Take the skillet from the flame and, if needed, drain any excess grease. Return the skillet to medium flame, then whisk in the dried basil, crushed tomatoes, tomato sauce, and oregano. Simmer the sauce for approximately ten minutes on medium or medium-low flame.
3. Once the noodles are done cooking, drain and return to the pot. Whisk in the cream cheese immediately, then toss the noodles with tongs until mostly melted. Whisk in the cottage cheese, ½ cup of Parmesan cheese, and ½ cup of mozzarella cheese. Toss the noodles until they are completely coated. Whisk in two cups of the red sauce. Keep the rest of the red sauce warm on the stove.
4. Scrape the noodles into the heated pie platter, then press them evenly into the dish with a flat spatula until they are firmly pressed together and equally flat on the surface. Distribute the remaining ¼ cup of Parmesan and ¼ cup of mozzarella cheese across the top.
5. Bake the spaghetti pie for 20-22 minutes, or until hot and bubbly and the cheese is golden on top. Allow the dish to rest for ten minutes. Cut into slices and serve with the remaining red sauce.

98. MINI DUTCH APPLE PIES

Total Time: 55 Mins

Serving: 24

Ingredients

- 2 Pillsbury ready-made pie dough

For Apple Filling

- 3 fuji apples (peeled, cored, diced)
- ½ lemon
- ½ cup of granulated sugar
- ¼ cup of packed light brown sugar
- 3 tbsp flour
- 1 tbsp apple butter
- ground cinnamon, to taste
- ¼ tsp nutmeg, to taste

For Topping

- ¾ cup of flour
- ¼ cup of granulated sugar
- ¼ cup of packed light brown sugar
- ⅓ cup of firm butter

Directions

1. Warm the oven to 400 degrees.
2. Using a cupcake tin, set aluminum foil strips into each cupcake cup so that the ends are sticking out (this will help for pulling pies out of the pan). Sprinkle it with baking spray.
3. Roll out the chilled pie dough. Cut out twenty-four circles with a "1 cup" size measuring cup.
4. In the cup, press the dough circles.
5. In a big bowl, mix diced apples and juice of ½ lemon. Combine the sugar, flour, spices, and apple butter.
6. In another bowl, with a pastry blender or a fork, mix the sugars, flour, and butter until coarsely crumbly.
7. To the top, fill each pie crust with apples. Distribute the topping over the apples evenly.

8. Bake for thirty to thirty-five minutes or until. Let cool completely prior to serving for the pie to set.

99. PINEAPPLE TARTS RECIPE

Prep Time: 30 Mins

Cook Time: 20 Mins

Total Time: 50 Mins

Serving: 140 Pieces

Ingredients

- 250 g butter
- 40 g icing sugar
- 2 egg yolks
- 1 tsp vanilla essence
- 350 g plain flour
- 20 g corn flour
- extra yolk for egg wash

Instructions

1. Warm the oven to 160 degrees Celsius.
2. Blend the butter and icing sugar until creamy.
3. Combine the vanilla paste/essence and egg yolk.
4. Mix well again with the whisk.
5. Combine corn flour and plain flour.
6. Use a spatula to mix until it's just combined.
7. Press out the dough with a nastar mould.
8. Put pineapple jam in the middle and roll up to cover the jam.
9. Massage with the egg wash.
10. Bake for approximately fifteen to twenty minutes.

(PUDDINGS RECIPES)

100. EASY CHOCOLATE PUDDING

Prep Time: 5 Mins

Cook Time: 9 Mins

Total Time: 2 Hrs 30 Mins

Servings: 2 To 3

Ingredients

Chocolate Pudding for Two

- ¼ cup of granulated sugar
- 2 tbsp cornstarch
- ⅛ tsp salt
- 1½ cups of milk whole preferred (but any percentage is fine)
- ½ cup of chopped semisweet chocolate
- ½ tsp vanilla extract

Toppings

- whipped cream (optional)
- chocolate shavings (optional)

Instructions

1. In a 2-quart saucepan, stir sugar, cornstarch, and salt. Gently stir in milk, whisking out any lumps as they form.
2. Warm over a medium-low flame, whisking every other minute or so, until the combination is thick enough to coat the back of a spoon (eight to twelve minutes). If the combination starts to simmer before it gets thick, lower the flame a bit.
3. Whisk in the chocolate until completely incorporated, about 1 to 2 minutes. Stir in the vanilla.
4. To take any lumps, strain the pudding through a fine mesh strainer. Put into individual serving cups or a single container and let cool for at least fifteen minutes at room temperature. Wrap with plastic wrap--if you're concerned about pudding skin, place the wrap directly on the surface--and chill for two to three hours until set.
5. If preferred, top with whipped cream and chocolate shavings, and enjoy!

101. YORKSHIRE PUDDINGS RECIPES

Prep Time: 5 Mins

Cook Time: 20 Mins

Total Time: 25 Mins

Servings: 2-4

Ingredients

- 1 egg
- 50g plain flour
- 4 tbsp milk
- 1 tbsp sunflower oil

Instructions

1. In a small jug or bowl, combine the flour and egg and mix until smooth. Add the milk one tbsp at a time, mixing thoroughly until the batter is lump-free. Season well with salt and pepper. It can be made up to one hour ahead and set aside at room temp or covered and chilled for up to four hours.
2. Set the oven temperature to 230C/210C fan/gas 8. Split the sunflower oil evenly between two holes of a Yorkshire pudding tin or four holes of a nonstick muffin tin and warm in the oven. When the oil is warm, slowly and evenly put the batter into the prepared holes. Bake for twenty to twenty-five minutes without opening the oven door, until the puddings puff up and brown. Serve right away. Once completely cooled, it will stay frozen for up to a month.

102. BREAD PUDDING

Prep Time: 15 Mins

Cook Time: 45 Mins

Total Time: 1 Hr

Servings: 12

Ingredients

- 6 slices of day-old bread (torn into small pieces)
- 2 tbsp unsalted melted butter
- ½ cup of raisins (optional)
- 2 cups of milk
- ¾ cup of white sugar
- 4 large beaten eggs
- 1 tsp ground cinnamon
- 1 tsp vanilla extract

Directions

1. Warm the oven to 350 degrees Fahrenheit/175 degrees Celsius.
2. Put the bread pieces in an 8-inch square baking pan. Sprinkle melted butter over the bread, then distribute with raisins.
3. In a medium mixing bowl, stir milk, sugar, eggs, cinnamon, and vanilla until thoroughly blended. Put the combination over the bread and gently press down with a fork until it is completely covered and soaked up the liquid.
4. Bake in the warmed oven until golden brown and the top springs back once lightly pressed, for about forty-five minutes.

103. EASY RICE PUDDING

Total Time: 40 Mins

Servings: 6

Ingredients

- ¾ cup of medium-grain white rice
- 1½ cups of water
- ½ tsp salt
- 2 cups of milk
- 1 egg
- ¼ cup of sugar
- 2 tbsp butter
- ½ tsp vanilla extract

Instructions

1. In a big saucepan, put water to a boil. Put back to a boil, then add the rice and salt. Cover and cook for approximately fifteen to twenty minutes, or until water is absorbed, over a simmer with a tight-fitting lid.
2. Increase the heat to medium-low, add milk, and cook until thick and creamy, stirring continually; approximately fifteen to twenty minutes.
3. In a small bowl, stir the eggs. Add 1-2 tbsp of the hot liquid to the egg, whisking continuously. When whisked in, add 1-2 tbsp of the hot liquid to the egg, whisking continuously. Repeat if required, thoroughly whisking after each addition until the egg combination has warmed.
4. Gently stir the egg and sugar combination into the rice and milk combination. Cook for another two to three minutes. Take from the flame and whisk in the butter and vanilla extract.

104. BANANA PUDDING (FROM SCRATCH)

Prep Time: 10 Mins

Cook Time: 15 Mins

Chill Time: 1 Hr

Total Time: 1 Hr 25 Mins

Servings: 4

Ingredients

Vanilla Pudding

- 1⅓ cups of granulated sugar
- 6 tbsp cornstarch
- pinch salt
- 4 cups of whole milk
- 2 tbsp unsalted butter
- 2 tbsp vanilla extract
- 54 vanilla wafers
- 2 large bananas

Whipped Topping

- 1 cup of heavy whipping cream
- ¼ cup of powdered sugar

Instructions

1. To prepare the pudding, stir together the sugar, cornstarch, and salt in a pot.
2. Gently put in the milk, stirring with a rubber spatula until smooth.
3. Increase the flame to medium and cook until steaming, stirring continuously. (Do not boil; reduce the temp if necessary.)
4. Take the pudding from the flame when it has thickened into a pudding-like texture.
5. Whisk in the butter and vanilla extract. Let the pudding to cool fully while stirring it regularly. It'll thicken even more as it cools. Set aside.
6. Layer eighteen vanilla wafers in a glass loaf pan, then top with a sliced banana.
7. Sprinkle half of the pudding that has cooled. Top with another eighteen vanilla wafers and the last sliced banana. Sprinkle on the remaining pudding.
8. In a bowl, mix heavy whipping cream and powdered sugar to make the whipped topping.

9. Mix until the combination is fluffy with stiff peaks. Sprinkle whipped topping on top of the pudding combination.
10. Put the last vanilla wafers on top in a neat line. Put in the fridge for one hour. Serve cold.

105. VANILLA PUDDING RECIPES

Prep Time: 5 Mins

Cook Time: 20 Mins

Cool Time: 20 Mins

Total Time: 45 Mins

Servings: 4

Ingredients

- ½ cup of whole milk
- 2 tbsp sugar
- ⅛ tsp salt
- ¼ cup of heavy cream or heavy whipping cream
- 1 tbsp cornstarch
- ½ tbsp butter
- ¼ tsp vanilla extract
- optional toppings: whipped cream and fresh berries

Instructions

1. Put the milk into a 1-quart saucepan set over a medium-low flame. Whisk in the sugar and salt. Cook, stirring constantly, for approximately five minutes or until the combination starts to steam. In a small bowl, whisk together the cream and cornstarch until very smooth while the milk is heating.
2. To the boiling milk, add the cornstarch mixture and cook, stirring continually, until the combination begins to simmer.
3. Increase the flame to low and whisk for five minutes until the pudding has thickened.
4. Take the pan from the flame and add the butter and vanilla. Continue stirring until the butter is melted. To cool, put it into a bowl. Cover and put in the fridge until it's cold.
5. If preferred, top with berries and whipped cream.

106. SMALL BATCH CHEESECAKE

Preparation: 35 Mins

Cooking: 45 Mins

Chill Time: 3 Hrs 40 Mins

Total Time: 5 Hrs

Serving: 5

Ingredients

For Crust

- 1⅓ cups of graham cracker crumbs
- 3 tbsp unsalted melted butter
- 1 tbsp granulated sugar

For Cheesecake

- 16 Ounces full-fat softened cream cheese to room temperature
- ½ cup of granulated sugar
- 1 large egg, room temperature
- 1 tsp pure vanilla extract
- 1 tsp fresh lemon juice

Instructions

1. Increase the oven rack to the third position and warm to 325 degrees Fahrenheit. Line a 9-by5-inch loaf pan with parchment paper, allowing enough overhang on the sides. Set aside.

Crust

2. Combine graham cracker crumbs, unsalted butter, and granulated sugar. Put into the prepared loaf pan and press down to form the crust. Compact it down with a flat spatula.
3. Bake the crust for twenty-two to twenty-four minutes or until softly golden brown at the edges and top.

Cheesecake

4. Combine the cream cheese on high speed in a big bowl using a hand blender or a stand blender with a paddle attachment until it is completely smooth.

5. For about two minutes, or until smooth and well combined, beat in the sugar, egg, vanilla, and lemon juice. If you need to, scrape the sides and bottom of the bowl and beat again.
6. Put the batter on top of the warm crust and smooth into an even layer.
7. Bake the cheesecake for forty to forty-five minutes or until the surface is completely set. In the middle of the cheesecake, a toothpick should come out largely clean.
8. Take the pan from the oven and set it on a wire rack to chill fully. When cooled, refrigerate the cheesecake for four hours or up to one day.
9. Using the overhang on the sides, take the chilled cheesecake from the pan.
10. Slice and serve with optional toppings, then enjoy!

107. APPLE TURNOVERS

Prep Time: 30 Mins

Cook Time: 20 Mins

Total Time: 50 Mins

Servings: 4

Ingredients

- 1 batch of 15-minute puff pastry
- 2 cups of diced apples
- 1 tsp ground cinnamon
- 1 tbsp freshly squeezed lemon juice
- 1 tbsp unsalted butter
- ¼ cup of light brown sugar
- pinch of salt
- 1 large beaten egg yolk
- coarse sugar for sprinkling (optional)

Instructions

1. Warm the oven to 400 degrees Fahrenheit and prepare a big cooking sheet with parchment paper.
2. First, peel and core the apples, and then dice them. You should have two cups of diced apples. Some less is fine.

3. To a sauté pan, add the apples, cinnamon, lemon juice, sugar, butter, and salt. Cook over medium flame for approximately seven minutes or until the apples soften and caramelize. Whisk frequently.
4. Take the apples from the flame and let them cool.
5. In the meanwhile, roll the dough into a 12-inch square. To prevent sticking, sprinkle flour as you go.
6. Split the apple combination into four piles in the corners of the dough, leaving about ¾" of border. Slice the dough into four equal squares. Over each of the apple piles, fold the dough's edges. You will have four triangular pies.
7. Use your fingers and fork tines to crimp the edges closed.
8. Slowly move the pies to the baking sheet.
9. Massage each pie generously with beaten egg yolk. If using, distribute with coarse sugar.
10. Bake for twenty minutes or until the pies are golden brown and puffy. Serve right away.

108. SMALL BATCH BROWN BUTTER CHOCOLATE CHIP COOKIES

Prep Time: 30 Mins

Cook Time: 12 Mins

Total Time: 42 Mins

Servings: 13

Ingredients

- 55 grams unsalted brown butter
- ¼ cup of sunflower or grapeseed oil
- 1 tbsp water
- 1 tbsp real vanilla extract
- 1 big egg (doesn't need to be room temperature)
- ⅔ cup of light brown sugar
- ¼ cup of granulated sugar
- 1 tsp baking powder
- ½ tsp baking soda
- ½ tsp sea salt
- 1½ cups of all-purpose flour
- ¾ cup of coarsely chopped dark chocolate

Instructions

For the Brown Butter

1. In a small saucepan, warm five tbsp butter over medium flame. When melted, crank up the flame to medium-high. Stand by, constantly stirring and watching. Small golden bits will begin to settle on the bottom of the pan. When this happens, take it off the flame and put it into a medium, heat-safe bowl to cool until closer to room temp but still liquid.

For the Cookie Dough

2. When the butter has cooled, stir in the sunflower oil, water, vanilla, and egg until well incorporated and the color has lightened, approximately one to two minutes. Stir in the brown sugar, sugar, baking powder, baking soda, and salt for approximately 1 minute until combined. Fold in the flour with a spatula until it is just mixed and there are still small flour streaks visible. Finally, fold in the chocolate chips until well distributed throughout the dough. Put the dough in the fridge for twenty minutes with a piece of plastic wrap on top of it.
3. Set the oven temp to 350 degrees F (177°C). Use parchment paper to cover your baking sheets. Put three tbsp of dough on the ready baking sheet, leaving approximately two ½-inches between dough balls.
4. Bake in the middle of the oven for about twelve minutes or until the edges are golden and the middle is a little underbaked. Distribute with sea salt flakes (optional) and cool thoroughly on the baking sheet prior to serving.

109. SMALL BATCH MUDDY BUDDIES RECIPE

Prep Time: 8 Mins

Cook Time: 2 Mins

Total Time: 10 Mins

Servings: 4

Ingredients

- 2 tbsp salted butter
- ⅓ cup of creamy peanut butter
- ⅔ cup of semisweet chocolate chips
- ½ tsp vanilla extract

- 3 cups of rice Chex cereal
- 1½ cups of powdered sugar

Instructions

1. In a large microwave-safe bowl, warm butter, peanut butter, and chocolate chips for sixty to ninety seconds, stirring every twenty to thirty seconds until smooth. Whisk in the vanilla extract.
2. To coat, add Chex cereal to the melted chocolate combination and swirl slowly with a rubber spatula.
3. Fill a big Ziplock bag with powdered sugar and the chocolate-covered Chex cereal combination. Seal tightly, then shake vigorously until everything is evenly coated in powdered sugar.

110. EASY SMALL BATCH FOCACCIA

Prep Time: 15 Mins

Cook Time: 35 Mins

Proofing Time: 1 Hr 45 Mins

Servings: 6

Ingredients

- 1 tsp yeast
- 1 tsp sugar
- 1¼ cups of water
- 2 ½ cups of flour
- ½ tbsp kosher salt
- 2 tbsp olive oil + extra for greasing and drizzle

Instructions

1. Mix together one tsp of yeast, one tsp sugar, and 1¼ cups of water into a big bowl and let sit for five to ten minutes until the combination gets foamy.
2. To make a shaggy dough, add 2½ cups of flour and ½ tbsp kosher salt and mix until the flour is hydrated.
3. Put two tbsp of olive oil over the dough and turn to coat it. Wrap it with plastic wrap and let it to rise until doubled (approximately one hour in a 100°F oven, two hours on the counter at ambient temperature, or eight to twenty-four hours in the fridge).

4. Use a lot of olive oil to grease the inside of an 8x8-inch baking pan. Deflate the dough and move it to the prepared pan. Allow it to rise until it has filled the pan (depending on the temp of the dough, this will take forty-five minutes if proofed at 100°F and up to 4 hours coming out of the refrigerator).
5. Warm the oven to 450°F, with the rack in the center.
6. Sprinkle the dough with olive oil prior to baking, then dimple it with your oiled hands. Distribute with salt and bake until it's deep golden in color, approximately thirty-five minutes. Allow to cool in the pan for at least fifteen minutes prior to turning it out; it's best served warm from the oven.

111. SMALL BATCH BROWNIES RECIPE

Prep Time: 15 Mins

Cook Time: 20 Mins

Total Time: 35 Mins

Servings: 8

Ingredients

- 2 ounces bittersweet or semi-sweet chocolate chips
- ¼ cup of cubed salted butter
- ½ cup of minus 1 tbsp granulated sugar
- 2 tbsp packed light brown sugar
- 1 large egg room temperature
- 1 tsp vanilla
- ½ cup of spooned and leveled all-purpose flour
- 2 tbsp sifted Dutch process cocoa powder
- ¼ cup of semi-sweet chocolate chips (optional)
- Flakey sea salt for sprinkling on top

Instructions

1. Warm the oven to 325° F. Sprinkle nonstick baking spray on a 9x5-inch loaf pan and set parchment paper on the bottom and sides. Let the parchment edges to hang an inch or two over the pan's edges for easy removal of the baked brownies.
2. In a double boiler over a low flame, warm the chocolate and butter together. Whisk frequently until smooth and shiny. Alternatively, warm the chocolate and butter in the microwave for 30 seconds at 50% power.

3. When melted, add the sugars and stir until well combined. Set aside to cool a bit.
4. Put the egg and vanilla and stir to combine well. Shiny and smooth, the batter will be.
5. Combine the flour and cocoa powder (and salt, if using unsalted butter). Use a big spatula to fold the batter together, taking care not to overmix. Whisk until only a few streaks of flour and cocoa remain.
6. If using, fold in the chocolate chips.
7. Move the batter to the prepared loaf pan.
8. Bake for 20-22 minutes, or until the edges are firm and a toothpick introduced an inch or two from the pan edge comes out clean or with a few crumbs.
9. Take it from the oven and let it cool on a wire rack prior to cutting it into squares.
10. Distribute with flakey sea salt prior to serving if desired.

112. EASY SMALL BATCH BROWNIES RECIPE

Prep Time: 10 Mins

Cook Time: 25 Mins

Total Time: 35 Mins

Servings: 8

Ingredients

- 4 tbsp butter
- 1 tbsp oil vegetable or canola
- ⅓ cup of granulated sugar
- ¼ cup of brown sugar
- 1 egg
- 1 tsp vanilla extract
- ¼ tsp salt
- ¼ cup of all-purpose flour
- ⅓ cup of cocoa powder
- ¼ cup of chocolate chunks
- sea salt flakes for topping

Instructions

1. Begin by preheating the oven to 325F, then line a 9x5 or 8x5 baking pan with parchment paper and set aside.
2. In a big bowl, warm the butter and oil in the microwave or on the stovetop in a medium saucepan.
3. If you melt the butter in a saucepan, move it to a big bowl; if not, simply add the granulated sugar and brown sugar to the butter and stir until thoroughly combined.
4. Put in the egg and the vanilla and stir to combine. Stir in the flour, cocoa powder, and salt until the flour combination disappears. Fold in the chocolate chunks, then put the brownie batter into the baking pan. Sprinkle the brownie batter evenly over the loaf pan and bake for twenty-five minutes in the heated oven.
5. Once you insert a toothpick into the center and it comes out with only a few wet crumbs, you'll know your brownies are done. Let the brownies to cool completely prior to cutting into them and enjoying!

113. SMALL BATCH CHEX MIX

Prep Time: 10 Mins

Cook Time: 1 Hr

Cool Time: 20 Mins

Total Time: 1 Hr 30 Mins

Serving: 4 ½

Ingredients

- 1 cup of corn Chex cereal
- 1 cup of rice Chex cereal
- 1 cup of wheat Chex cereal
- ½ cup of mixed nuts
- ½ cup of mini pretzels
- ½ cup of bagel chips
- 2 tbsp melted butter (dairy-free stick butter will also work)
- 2-3 tsp Worcestershire sauce
- ½-¾ tsp season salt
- ¼ tsp garlic powder
- ⅛-¼ tsp onion powder

Instructions

1. Warm the toaster oven at 250°F on the BAKE setting, then lower the cooking rack.
2. In a big bowl, combine the cereals, mixed nuts, pretzels, and bagel chips.
3. Put the butter in a small microwave-safe bowl and microwave for approximately twenty seconds until melted. Whisk in the Worcestershire sauce, seasoned salt, garlic powder, and onion powder.
4. Put butter combination over cereal and whisk well to coat all of the pieces.
5. Put combine into a small roasting pan or rimmed sheet pan.
6. Bake for one hour, whisking every fifteen minutes during cooking.
7. Sprinkle the mixture on paper towels or parchment paper and let it cool fully (about fifteen to twenty minutes) prior to storing it in an airtight container.

114. PEANUT BUTTER ENERGY BALLS (AKA QUICK AND HEALTHY SNACK BITES)

Total Time: 20 Mins

Servings: 3 Dozen

Ingredients

- 1 cup of quick-cooking oats
- 1 cup of coconut flakes
- ½ cup of natural, crunchy peanut butter
- 3 ½ tbsp honey
- ¼ cup of ground flaxseed meal
- ¼ cup of toasted wheat germ
- 1 tsp vanilla
- ¼ cup of mini chocolate chips

Instructions

1. In a medium bowl, mix each ingredient except the chocolate chips.
2. Whisk to combine.
3. Add chocolate chips to the combination and stir until just combined.
4. To form one-inch balls, firmly press with your hands.
5. Put in an airtight container and refrigerate when needed.

115. SMALL-BATCH VANILLA CUPCAKES

Prep Time: 10 Mins

Cook Time: 16 Mins

Total Time: 1 Hr

Servings: 6

Ingredients

Small-Batch Vanilla Cupcakes

- 3 tbsp unsalted softened butter
- ¼ cup and 3 tbsp granulated sugar
- 1 large egg white
- ½ tsp vanilla extract
- ½ cup of all-purpose flour measured (using the spoon and sweep method and divided)
- ½ tsp baking powder
- ⅛ tsp salt
- ¼ cup and 1 tbsp milk

Vanilla Buttercream

- 4 tbsp unsalted softened butter
- 1 cup of sifted powdered sugar
- 1 tsp to 1 tbsp milk or cream
- ¼ tsp vanilla extract
- pinch of salt
- sprinkles (optional)

Instructions

Small-Batch Vanilla Cupcakes

1. Warm the oven to 375°F and prepare a cupcake tray with six liners.
2. Blend the sugar and butter in a medium bowl with a handheld electric blender for about one to two minutes or until light and fluffy.
3. Combine the egg white and vanilla. Mix on medium until smooth.
4. Combine baking powder, ¼ cup of flour, and salt. And mix on low until combined.

5. Mix in the milk on low. Mix in the remaining ¼ cup of flour on medium until well combined and smooth. Split batter between prepared cupcake cups, filling just under ⅔ full. This will make exactly six cupcakes. Bake for approximately seventeen to twenty minutes, until a toothpick introduced into the middle of the cupcakes comes out clean or with a few dried crumbs.
6. Once the cupcakes are chill enough to handle, move them to a cooling rack and let to cool fully prior to icing.

Vanilla Buttercream

7. In a medium bowl, mix powdered sugar, butter, milk or cream, vanilla, and salt. If necessary, add ½ tsp of milk and beat until the frosting comes together.
8. Move frosting to a piping bag and pipe it over cupcakes, or distribute it with a knife. If desired, top with distributes and enjoy!

116. SMALL-BATCH VANILLA CAKE

Prep Time: 10 Mins

Cook Time: 20 Mins

Cool Time: 10 Mins

Total Time: 40 Mins

Servings: 4

Ingredients

- 7 tbsp unsalted butter
- ½ cup of granulated sugar
- ½ tsp vanilla extract
- 2 medium eggs
- ⅞ cup of self-rising flour

Instructions

1. Set the oven's temperature to 375°F, or 190°C. Grease a 6-inch baking tin.
2. Put sugar, butter, and vanilla extract into a bowl and blend it well until the consistency is creamy and lump-free.
3. Beat the eggs in one at a time.
4. Finally, fold in the self-rising flour and combine thoroughly.
5. Put the batter into the baking tin and set it in the oven.

6. Bake for twenty to twenty-five or until risen and golden brown on top. When gently pushed in the center, the cake should begin to pull away from the sides of the pan and spring back. A toothpick introduced in the center will come out with only one or two little crumbs.
7. Let the cake chill in its pan for ten minutes, then turn it out onto a wire rack and let it cool fully.

117. HOT MILK SPONGE CAKE

Total Time: 30 Mins

Servings: 2

Ingredients

For the Cake

- 70 g plain all-purpose flour
- ½ tsp baking powder
- pinch of salt
- ¼ cup of whole-fat milk
- ½ tbsp butter
- ½ tsp vanilla extract
- 1 large free-range egg
- 100 g granulated sugar

To Top and Fill

- 2 cups of fresh strawberries
- 1 tbsp strawberry jam
- ½ cup of whipping cream whipped until stiff
- icing sugar to dust

Instructions

1. Set the oven temp to 350°F (180°C), or gas mark 4. Line a nine-by-four-inch loaf pan with cooking paper and butter it.
2. To melt the butter, warm the milk and butter in the microwave for approximately thirty seconds.
3. Whisk in the vanilla. Set aside.
4. Sift the flour, baking powder, and salt. Set aside.

5. Mix the egg and sugar together until the volume doubles and the beaters form a ribbon when taken from the bowl.
6. Add the flour combination alternating with the milk, making three dry and two wet additions, mixing well, but trying to not knock any air from the eggs.
7. Put into the ready baking tin.
8. Bake in a heated oven for twenty to twenty-five minutes or until risen and golden brown.
9. Leave in the tin for approximately five minutes and next unmold onto a wire rack to cool fully.
10. If you are filling with berries and cream: Rinse and slice your berries, then crush half of them. Mix together in a bowl with the jam and set aside for a few minutes while you whip the cream.
11. Whip the cream with or without a sprinkle of sugar until it is thick and retains its form.
12. Gently slice the cake into two lengthwise pieces. Put one piece, cut side up, on a serving platter. Top with half of the berries. Dollop the cream on top and put the other half of the cake, right side up, over the cream.
13. Distribute with icing sugar and serve with the remaining berries on the side.

118. SMALL CHOCOLATE CAKE

Prep Time: 10 Mins

Cook Time: 29 Mins

Total Time: 39 Mins

Servings: 9

Ingredients

- 1¾ cups of flour
- ⅓ cup of Dutch cocoa powder
- ½ tsp baking soda
- 1 ½ tsp baking powder
- 1¼ cups of granulated sugar
- ⅓ cup of vegetable oil
- 2 eggs
- ½ cup of buttermilk
- ⅔ cup of hot coffee

- 1 tsp vanilla extract
- ⅓ tsp salt

For the Chocolate Frosting

- 200 g butter
- 60 g melted and cooled dark chocolate
- 1¼ cups of powder sugar
- ⅓ cup of cocoa powder
- ½ tsp kosher salt
- 1 tsp vanilla extract
- 2-4 tbsp milk

Instructions

1. Set the oven temp to 180°C (350°F) and line an 8-by-8-inch cake pan with parchment paper.
2. In a large mixing bowl, put the eggs, vegetable oil, sugar, vanilla extract, salt, buttermilk, and cocoa powder. Mix with a stir until well combined.
3. Put the baking soda, flour, baking powder, and hot coffee, and mix with a stir until well mixed.
4. Put the mixture into the ready baking pan and bake in a 180 degrees Celsius (350f) heated oven for about thirty minutes or until a toothpick introduced in the cake comes out clean.

Make the chocolate buttercream

5. Into a big mixing bowl, put the cooled dark chocolate, kosher salt, soft butter, powdered sugar, heavy cream, and vanilla extract, and sift in the cocoa powder. Mix until the frosting comes together on low speed.
6. Increase the speed to medium to high and mix for approximately three minutes or until the frosting is silky smooth.
7. Put the frosting on top of the cake that is at room temperature and use a spoon to make waves.

119. COCONUT COOKIE BARS

Prep Time: 10 Mins

Cook Time: 30 Mins

Total Time: 40 Mins

Servings: 8

Ingredients

- ½ cup of melted butter
- 1 cup of soft light brown sugar
- 1 large free-range egg
- ½ tbsp vanilla
- 1 cup of plain all-purpose flour
- pinch salt
- 1¼ cups of divided shredded sweetened coconut
- scant cup of dark, bittersweet, or semi-sweet chocolate chips

Instructions

1. Set the oven temp to 350°F (180°C) or gas mark 4. Butter an 8-inch square baking tray and line it with baking paper, leaving enough overhang to pull the squares out once cold.
2. Put the brown sugar and melted butter in a bowl and beat them together until they are well mixed. Combine the egg and vanilla. Whisk in the salt.
3. Gently add the flour until it is thoroughly combined. Whisk in 1 cup of coconut and chocolate chips.
4. Sprinkle the dough into the ready baking tin evenly, leveling it off. Distribute the remaining coconut over the top.
5. Bake in the heated oven for thirty minutes (mine took an extra five minutes) or until the edges are golden brown and the middle is set. Leave it to cool in the tin prior to lifting it out and slicing it into bars.

THE END

Printed in Great Britain
by Amazon